# Dad Dedications

## A Collection of Poetry

### Edited by Annabel Cook

First published in Great Britain in 2005 by
Young Writers, Remus House, Coltsfoot Drive
Peterborough PE2 9JX
Telephone: 01733 890066
Website: www.youngwriters.co.uk

# Foreword

The book you are about to read is a heartfelt and youthful tribute to fatherhood. A competition was held to coincide with Father's Day, to give children and teenagers who enjoy poetry the opportunity to not only have their work published, but also to show how they feel for their dads. Be they thankful, emotional or humorous, these poems are sure to warm any heart, father or not, and are certain to be a welcome addition to your family bookshelf.

# Contents

# The Poems

# No Stranger

The whispers of a morning chill,
Shudder through the air,
A vision of a lonesome child,
Whom no one gives a care,
Lies amongst the debris,
Of a bitter life so cold,
The remains of once a happy dream,
Are battered, worn and old.

But suddenly some hope appears,
A candle in the night,
This hero needs no shiny shield,
Or vicious sword, to fight.
He takes my hand and leads me home,
Who is this man I see?
A rescuer he truly is,
A man who resembles me.

*Daniella McLenaghan (14)*

Congratulations Daniella!
From our selection of prizes
you chose to give your dad a
replica Manchester United
football shirt for Father's Day.

# Dad In A Million

I love my dad very much,
More than words can say.
He's always with me in my thoughts,
I love him more each day.
If I could choose who my dad was,
I wouldn't change a thing.
Because of all the dads in the world,
I think he is the king.
Camping trips and other treats
And holidays galore,
I'm happy that he is my dad,
I couldn't ask for more.
I think about him every day
And I know it's true,
That every day, no matter what,
Dad, I'll always love you!

Hannah Price (11)

# My Dad!

I call him a name,
A very special name,
A name that I call no one else.

Here's why ...

He makes me feel safe,
When no one else can,
That's why I call him that name.

He makes me laugh,
When I really want to cry,
That's why I call him that name.

I love him very much,
And he loves me,
That's why I call him that name.

The name I call him is Dad,
And he deserves that name in every way.

Helen Matheson (11)

# My Dad's Famous ...

My dad's a boxer,
The best I have seen,
He's tough and he's hard,
He's strong and he's lean.
My dad's a singer,
He's hit number 1,
He's won 'Pop Idol'
Five times, in a run.
My dad's a racer,
In the Grand Prix
He lifted the cup,
In 2003.
My dad's a dancer
In big West End shows,
He also does ballet,
He's got dancing toes.
My dad's an artist,
He paints all the time,
He could be famous,
But chose to be mine.

Emma Jacobs (12)

# Something Special

I close my eyes and take a deep breath,
I never meant what I just said.
I am ashamed and I dare not look up to see
The look of horror that looks back at me.

But instead you just smile, pat me gently then walk away,
Telling me I should be more careful about what I say.
Dumbstruck, I mumble an apology.
Thinking, *how can he forgive me so easily?*
But you are my father and you understand me.
Therefore, you know what I say I don't always mean,
No matter how real it may seem.

But you are something special and sacred to me,
A priceless gift from wherever it may be.
So I am writing this poem to tell you,
That no matter what I say or do,
I will always love you.

*Chorin Kawa (15)*

# My Dad

To have a dad just like you,
Is to have a guardian angel all my life through,
To love and protect me, I admire and respect,
I just hope I live up to what you expect.

I just want you to know,
You mean the world to me,
Only a heart as pure as yours,
Would give so unselfishly.

The things you've done,
Every time you're there,
Gives me knowledge inside,
To see how much you really care.

Friends I can choose,
Relatives I'm stuck with,
But as my relative, my friend,
I'm glad, I love you no end.

Even though I may not say,
I am grateful for all you do,
I am blessed in having such a fun-loving dad,
A dad, my dad, that's you!

Joanne Healey (16)

# Untitled

The day I was born, you first loved me,
Holding me in your arms, a tiny little girl was all you coul
Protecting me from the big world, too little to understan
You guided me through life, and always held my hand.
Now I'm a big girl, I can face the world alone,
Falling in love, and one day leaving home.
But you'll always be my father,
Now and forever after.

*Rebecca Wright*

TOP
10

# A Poem For Dad

I was only a lad when it happened,
You were ill and there was nothing you could do.
A tumour, they said, a benign one at that,
Why did it have to be you?

A new job for me, I was the man of the house,
What a hard job it was going to be.
Cuddling Mummy whenever she felt sad,
Sometimes she had to cuddle me.

You beat the tumour and that was fine,
We were relieved and glad to have you back.
Until disaster struck, you fell ill again,
This time a heart attack.

'What did I do to deserve this?'
I kept saying over in my head.
I was sad, lonely, depressed and angry,
To see you lying in that bed.

The years went by, we stuck together,
Through the good times and through the bad.
Sometimes I think I missed out on things,
Although sometimes I'm glad I have.

You give me hope and encouragement,
To be what I want to be.
You give me inspiration,
It means so much to me.

So Dad let me say, I'm glad you're my dad,
Your qualities are second to none.
I would like to say from the bottom of my heart,
I'm proud to be called your son.

*Ryan Gibb (18)*

# Untitled

Fishing, sailing, motor mad,
Makes me laugh, then makes me sad;
Backs up Mum when I've done wrong,
Aren't I just the lucky one!

Presents scattered round the tree,
From me to Dad, from Dad to me;
Gratitude flowing through the air,
Smiles and laughter everywhere.

Special memories mean so much,
And Dad's just got that special touch,
To soothe me down when I feel distressed,
To tell me how to look my best.

Traipsing round a hundred zoos,
Waiting in the theme park queues;
Sharing hobbies, swapping jokes,
Eating home-grown artichokes.

Thank you for the love you've shown,
You'll never leave me on my own;
So Dad, although we'll move apart,
You'll be forever in my heart.

*Victoria Brooks (14)*

# Untitled

My dad is a punk rocker
with a flash red guitar,
his eyes as blue as skies,
his hair as black as tar.

My dad is a famous footballer,
best friends with famous Dave.
He has played against Wayne Rooney
and every ball shot, he saves.

My dad's a famous jockey
he beat Dettori at Ascot.
Dad's horse is called Lightning,
he is the fastest England's got.

My dad is a fireman,
he rescued me from the flames.
He has been knighted by the Queen
for rescuing damsels and dames.

So, maybe my dad isn't all that,
he isn't famous you see
but the reason my dad is the best,
is because he loves me.

Fleur Wheatley (12)

# My Dad

My dad has travelled afar.
He has travelled by van and car.
My dad fixes things to make them right.
That's my dad, he thinks he's always right.
My dad is always there for us
To play and learn along with us.
I love my dad
He is the best
So here's to him
And all the rest.

Liam Ferguson (11)

# A Father Is ...

A father is someone funny.
A father is as sweet as honey.
A father is a kind person.
My father has a rare talent.
A father's heart is as big as an oak tree.
My father is the best dad in the world.

Jamie Egdell (10)

# My Father Is ...

A father is funny
A father is someone who'll play with your toys
When he gets the chance
A father is adventurous
A father is someone you can look up to
A father is faithful
He's equal, you could call him the share bear
A father is caring
He's not into football, he's not into sport
That's why I like him
A father is warm
He works in the house as quiet as a mouse
A father is kind
He feeds my tummy and loves my mummy
But never thinks of himself.

Gregory Seed (9)

# A Father Is ...

A father is ... someone you can rely on.
A father is ... a fun roller coaster.
A father is ... a person you can look up to.
A father is ... a person who is funny and has lots of money.
A father is ... a person who is kind and helpful in every single way.
A father is ... a person who helps you all day.

*Rachel Thornton (9)*

# A Father Is ...

A father is someone who is very funny
Someone who smells of honey!
A father is someone who buys you ice cream
And takes you to the park for a swing!
A father is someone who is like a huge teddy bear
Who jumps on top of you and gives you a scare!

Alice Mary Longstaff (10)

# My Father

My father is like a full moon,
Shining brighter than all the stars.

My dad's eyes are like a beautiful rainbow
And his heart, it never ends.

My dad is a selfless person,
He does everything I want to do,
Life would be pointless without my dad.

My father plays football with me,
He plays rugby, cricket, golf as well.
You can never be bored when my dad's around.

My dad is the *best* dad in the whole wide world!

Eamon Nugent-Doyle (10)

# My Father

A father is ... kind and loving and always caring but,
My father is ... always up for anything.
A father is ... a wise old owl
Who knows everything except how to sing.
My father is ... always talking about cars.
A father is ... an everlasting friend
Who is always there for you no matter what.
But most of all the thing I like about my dad is
That he's *always full of love and money!*

Leah Cloonan (10)

# My Father

My father is kind and caring like no other father.
My father always watches 'The Simpsons' with me on our TV.
My father likes chocolate
And especially likes playing football and golf with me.
My father is like a clown who makes people laugh all day.
My father is the moon who brightens up a dull day.
My father is fun to be with all day, every day
But best of all my father is the father of my dreams.

Michael Mather (10)

# My Father

A father is
A big cuddly bear,
He steals all my chocolate,
But will always care.

My father's eyes
Are as nice as looking at the horizon,
And his huge heart
Is as big as my 6ft brother Simon.

My father loves me,
And I love him,
And if someone offered me 6 million pounds for him
I would throw it in the bin.

My love for my father,
Is really huge,
And I wouldn't change him or that,
For the world.

Joseph Cassidy (10)

# My Dad

My dad is mad,
I am so glad,
My dad likes coffee,
He also likes toffee.

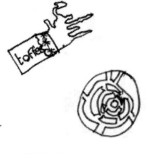

My dad likes 007,
And his favourite number is 11,
My dad is really cool,
I wouldn't trade him for a diamond stool.

My dad is really crazy,
He is also very lazy,
My dad likes sports,
But he lost his football shorts.

*Caspar Ward (10)*

# My Father

My father is ...
An eternal friend
My dad
Loves chocolate a lot.

My dad is a strict golfer
Or a valuable treasure
Never to be given up.

My father is ...
A man who can take you to an enjoyable place
Or a roller coaster that never ends.

My dad is ...
A wise, eternal owl
Or a top of the range car.

If he isn't any of those
Who cares?
He's still my dad.

Joseph Rafferty (10)

# My Father Is ...

A father is ... kind, gentle, caring
And cuddly like a bear.

A father is ... a wise owl
That twinkles in the night
Then the sun popping out in the daylight.

My father is ... a football
That scores right in the net.

My father is ... the green trees
And spreads the air to everyone.

My father is ... hot, warm, melted chocolate
With strawberries dipped in.

My father is ... the sunset
Then in the morning sends his light.

My father is ... honey
With quite a lot of money.

My father is ... love wrapped in a heart
And he sends it to me.

Alexandra Jones (10)

# My Father Is ...

My father is a cuddly bear
I cuddle him day and night.
My father is a crazy man
I think he is the craziest man in the world.
My father is so rare
No one will take him away from me.
My father is a kind man
He looks after me and he cares for me.
My father is mad about cars
He always knows everything about cars.
My father is the funniest and kindest man on Earth.

David Cross (10)

# My Dad

My dad is very kind,
He cares a lot for us.
He fixes things around the house,
And never makes a fuss.

He is very funny,
But sometimes he gets cross.
He tells me he's in charge,
But really Mum's the boss!

He makes up games for us to play,
But when he needs a rest,
I jump on his tummy.
Oh yes, my dad's the best!

Anna Chidlow (6)

# My Dad

My dad is such good fun,
He loves to play and run,
And when he finally catches me,
He likes to squeeze and tickle me.
My dad is number one!

Rachael Storey (6)

# Dad

Dad,
I know that I'm sometimes a pain,
Like the weather.
When they say it'll be sunny and then it rains.

When you've put your clothes out to dry,
And droplets fall from the sky,
And you have to start all over again.

Dad,
When I don't know what to do,
And you're there,
I feel grateful to have a father like you.

When illness dims the light,
You're there to help me fight,
And carry on to follow my route.

Dad,
No simile could ever describe you,
The way you are,
Anything you do.

A credit to the human race,
You will always have a special place,
In my heart.

Gurpreet Bharya (14)

# Poem For Dad

My dad is the best
Better than the rest
He works all day in the sun
Then he has a great icy bun

My dad has known me
For over 100 years
He's fed me, cleaned me
And wiped my tears

This poem may be short
But do I love him?
Yes, of course!

This is a poem just for him
So, Dad, if ya listening, come on in.

I love my dad ever so much.

Emma Harriet Scott (11)

# My Dad

Dads are an amazing thing
They impersonate Elvis and think they can sing.

They're either watching football or having a snooze
Or down the pub having a booze.

They're funny, happy, cheerful and kind
Although can be embarrassing at times.

Even though he burps, slurps and wears smelly socks
He is a great dad and I think he rocks.

*Dads are great!*

Tom Ludlow (11)

# Untitled

My dad is the best dad ever,
He goes to work feeling down in the dumps,
But he's still brave and strong!

My dad is the best dad ever,
He comes back from work feeling down in the dumps,
Because he hasn't had lots of luck selling machines,
But he is still brave and strong!

My dad is the best dad ever,
When he goes to bed he's *not* down in the dumps
Because he has his family around him.
My dad is the best dad ever!

Jack Pretious (10)

# My Dad

My dad is a giant
Not in a scary way
Just that he's really tall
That's what I mean to say

My dad is a wild bear
Not in a beastly way
Just he's really cuddly
That's what I mean to say

My dad is a cash machine
Not in a metal way
Just he gives me money
That's what I mean to say

My dad is a footy hooligan
Not in a crazy way
Just that he's a strong supporter
That's what I mean to say

My dad is just the best dad
Not much more to say
I just know I love him
In every possible way!

Shona Smith (12)

# Father Bear

Bear:
Sitting on my bedside table,
Looking very keen and able.
Dark brown, wistful eyes,
Like they hold a special surprise.
Soft, golden, weathered fur.

Father:
Mind of a philosopher,
Kind and brave, very strong,
Always right, sometimes wrong,
Dressed up smart, standing tall.
My pride comes before it all,
Dear Father Bear.

Geila Alpion (12)

# My Number One Dad

My number one dad is fantastic
He dearly adores me
He hugs, kisses and shows me affection
Also makes me feel special inside
My dad is like the sunshine
His smile is radiant and warm
My dad is my life!

Shannon Higginbotham (9)

# A Father's Day Poem

My dad's name is Peter
He has black hair and green eyes
It's fun being with my dad
He makes me happy all the time

My dad is a brave man
He is always there when I need him
He works very hard for my family
Dad took me lots of places around Europe

My daddy likes football
Sometimes he takes me to a match
I have a happy family
With Dad's helping hand

My dad is very polite
He is very tidy
Sometimes he washes the plates and dishes
Not a single toy on the floor

I love my dad
He could be very teasing
He plays with me
He is a very nice man.

Angelique De Raffaele (9)

*Dad Dedications*

# My Dad

My dad makes me smile,
Shall I tell you how?
By saying, 'Here, love, let me tie your lace,
Or better still let's have a race.'

My dad makes me smile,
Shall I tell you how?
By taking me to a shopping mall,
And buying me a dress fit for a ball.

My dad makes me smile,
Shall I tell you how?
By reading me fantastic tales,
His choice never fails.

My dad makes me smile,
Shall I tell you how?
By being *my dad!*

Aysha Patel (10)

# Dear Father

This is especially for you,
I hope you know I love you too,
You are the greatest dad in the world,
I don't care if your hair is curled,
The fact is you are my dad,
I suppose that is not all bad,
Ha, ha, ha, I got you then,
I bet you thought I was joking then
I hope you like Father's Day
So this gives me a chance to say,
I love you, Dad, you are great,
You are my best mate.
Happy Father's Day.

Megan Winsfield-Hill (11)

# Dad, I Love You!

Dad, I love you
When you tickle my toes
And rub my nose
Dad, I love you

Dad, I love you
From day and night
Especially when you hug me tight
Dad, I love you

Dad, I love you
You make me laugh
Because you're daft
Dad, I love you

Dad, I love you
With your enormous heart
You make things smart
I love you
'Cause you're my number one dad!

*Chloe Bilsbury (9)*

# A Father Is ...

A father is a grizzly bear
But doesn't have so much hair.
A father is loving and fair
And when I'm not well he gives me a pear.
A father is a funny dad
But sometimes he drives me mad.
A father is an old antique
And is very, very weak.
A father is special to me
Because he gives me sweeties.
My father is kind
I love my dad!

Eppie Beveridge (10)

# A Father Is ...

My father is kind and he makes me laugh,
Even though he never has a bath.
The bees are always on him like he's honey,
And he earns us all our money.
My father has grey hair,
And he's like a grizzly bear.
My father works hard all day,
And his birthday isn't in May.
My father is cool and kind,
And he always helps the blind.
My father is a cuddly toy,
And he acts like a little boy.
My father is cool,
And he plays pool.
My father is someone I'll never share,
And he will always be there.

Jay Turner (10)

# A Father Is ...

A father is the sun which brightens up a dark, gloomy day.
A father is an exciting roller coaster
Who chooses a new adventurous path every day.
A father is a cuddly bear
Who is always willing to have a hug.
A father is a chocolate chomper
Who occasionally (in top secret) pinches some lovely chocolate
And eats it.
A father is a wise owl who gives advice.
A father is an eternal friend.
*Best dad!*

*Jessica Dorr (9)*

# A Father Is ...

A father is ...
A huggable bear
Who makes you laugh
When no one is there!

A father is ...
A munching monster munch
Eating chocolate
Picking flowers in a bunch!

A father is ...
Someone special to look after you
When playing hide and seek
And comes out with a *boo!*

Amy Anderson (10)

# Poem For Dad

If I could choose from a million dads
I would certainly stick with the one I have
Sure, sometimes he makes me mad
But more importantly he makes me glad
My dad is very strong and tough
But this sensitive side is but enough
For I know when I hurt he will be there
To hold me and love me and show that he cares
I can cry all morning, all day and all night
And I can certainly with him cause a fight
But at the end of the day on him I can lean
And he wouldn't turn away even if I am mean
So to sum it all up about this wonderful man
Hmm, let me see, I will do the best I can
He's funny and kind and terribly sweet
But not always, like when my room isn't neat
'Oh look at your room, you can hardly close the door,
And pick up those clothes that are lying on the floor.'
So I sit and smile and nod my head
And pretend for a while I know what he said
Until it finally hits him I haven't a clue
What he's been saying hasn't gone through
We also discuss our personal lives
He asks me, 'How's the boyfriend?' I ask him, 'How's the wife?'
This is just a bit of how my dad can be
But I just have to say he's the only dad for me.

Kasendo Mbogori (14)

# Dads

Come in all shapes and sizes
Big ones
Small ones
Thin ones
Fat ones

Some have hair
Long
Short
Curly
Or fair

Some burp
Shout
Or swear

Some are funny
Some are sad
Sometimes they can be bad

But most of all I got my dad
My stepdad, he's not bad

He's big and bald
Round and fat
I just like him like that
My dad.

Chester Nixon (11)

# Dad

You get up early every day,
Off to work and school on the way.
You work hard all day 'til tea,
You're the best a dad could ever be.

You help people whose kidneys are broke,
And believe me, this is no joke.
Fix the machine, a kidney you've spared,
It's not just for me that you care.

You made me a tree house and a bed,
You iron my clothes and keep me fed.
You may be getting quite old,
But still you're clever, kind and bold.

You've always been there for me,
When I was little I'd sit on your knee.
You're only bad point is that you snore,
(I'm sure they hear it next door!)

I think of the things you and I have done,
All the family, we've had such fun.
I know you'll always be my dad,
For this I'll never be sad.

Claire Parsons (13)

# My New Dad Pete

I met a man
He is like a dad to me.
Some people say he's just a man
But I say he might be just a man to you
But he is my dad.
And that one you say is just a man
That is the one who makes me smile
When I did not think I could.
The one who said I can make it
When I did not believe I could.
The one who cared
When he did not have to.
So I say to my dad
To the best friend I ever had . .
. . . Thank you.
I thank God for giving me
A new dad and a best friend.

*Teri Harper (13)*

# I Don't See You Often, Dad

I do not see you often, but
I see you every day.
I've taken you along with me
As I have grown away.

We talk about the things that fill
A life with love and pain,
But our timeless golden time,
Unspoken, still remains.

You will always be my dad,
And I, your darling son.
The days may turn like waterwheels,
But that will never change.

The thought of you will make me glad
No matter where I wander.
You are the place that cannot feel
Uncanny, dark or strange.

Shanwayne Stephens (14)

# My Dad

My dad is a generous man
He's always helping others
He walks me to school in the morning
And chats to all the mothers.

He's always fun to be around
He always puts me first
My love for him is massive
Sometimes I want to burst.

We do fun things together
Like swimming, cycling and shopping
I help him in the garden
He lets me do the chopping.

Dad is really kind to me
He lets me stay up late
I love my dad millions
He is wonderful and great.

Daisy May Bonser (8)

# Dad, You've Always Been There

Dad, you've always been there
When I needed to confide
In someone who I could trust
And who's always on my side.

Dad, you've always been there
Whilst still working all the day
Building up my courage
Facing whatever comes your way.

Dad, you've always been there
To tell me right and wrong
Sometimes we did quarrel
Yet your love still goes strong.

Dad, you've always been there
Every hour of every day
Really I do love you
Despite what I might say.

Dad, you've always been there
Whenever you possibly could
Maybe we don't 'sing your praises'
As often as we should.

Dad, you've always been there
Through the thick and thin
If all the dads competed
You'd be sure to win!

Jessica Crawford (13)

# My Dad

He may not look the part
He may not wear suits and ties
Or run his own business
He only wears T-shirt and jeans
He may only work as a forklift driver
My dad may not have flash car
Or go to golf every Saturday
He likes to go fishing in the pouring rain
Or take a drive up the countryside
And get stuck in a puddle of mud
Let's just face facts
My dad's so strange
I think he is an alien
From outer space
But no matter where he's from
Or looks like
He'll always be my dad.

Kerry Johnson (12)

# Untitled

You may be the best
But you can be a pest.

You're careful and caring
And so good at sharing.

I know I am cheeky
And make you want to scream,
But you're still the best dad
I've ever seen.

Although you shout,
I love you so,
You make me smile,
You make me laugh.

Dad, you're the best
And that's a fact.

Sophie Mordue (12)

# Untitled

I've got this dad who's really friendly,
Who tucks me in bed very gently.
He works hard to make a living,
He's soft and warm and very forgiving.
So that is my dad,
My number one dad
And boy, am I glad
To have him around.

Aimee Wood (9)

# My Dad

Dad is always there for me,
He is wonderful as you will see,
He cares about me all the time,
Happy, gentle, safe and sublime,
Helping me with everything,
Wouldn't swap him for anything!

Bethany Perry (11)

# My Gold

The football you religiously observe
From early on you say Sky is reserved
The veg you show me, of which you are proud
The plants you tend to so happy and sound
Your swimming, when you are the fastest there
And the amount you swam is always shared
The sarcastic words that will 'toughen me up'
A poor excuse for your insults and stuff
The smell of wine on your breath at night
Can be smelt as you sleep, with eyes shut tight
The snoring and grumbles so clearly heard
Silence is golden and always preferred
These are the odd habits of which you hold
Please keep them always, to me they are gold.

*Jessica Richards (14)*

# Dad

Someone special, so loving, so caring,
A person who can be really daring.
An adult who hugs you when you are down,
They give a smashing smile to ease your frown.
This man helps you overcome your fears,
He always has a tissue to dry your tears.
When you go to bed he gives you a kiss,
This is a moment that feels so bliss.
If you are worried he listens to you,
Like a guardian angel seeing you through.

Who can this wonderful loved one be?
*My precious dad!*

*Bethany Hirons (11)*

# Untitled

My dad's a right laugh
He always wears a smile
He makes me really happy
With silly rhymes and jokes
But stinks the whole house with his egg yolks

When I'd got the hiccups
He'd turn me upside down!
And when I'm naughty
He'll give me a gentle frown!

I know how much he likes his coffee
But because what's left of his teeth will fall out
He doesn't touch toffee.

Lauren Morrison (12)

# My Dad

My dad can be embarrassing,
My dad can be mad,
My dad can be boring,
But still I love my dad.

My dad could work in a factory,
My dad could work down the lane,
My dad could work at my school,
But he will always be there, even if I am a pain.

My dad sings in public,
My dad sings loud and long,
My dad sings with the window open,
As his voice is very strong.

I love my dad because he is always there,
He always does his best,
He takes us on holiday all the way,
That's why I love my dad.

Katharine Millar (11)

# Only A Dad

Only a dad who loves me proud
Only a dad who would search around
Only a dad who would think I'm ace
Only a dad who would put a smile on my face!

Only a dad who would never ask for much
Just to try my best and to be a friend as such
Only a dad who could treat me true
Only a dad who would love me through and through

Only a dad who helps me with stuff
Only a dad who knows me well enough
Only a dad who I love too
Only a dad who can share this through

Only a dad who is as brilliant as mine
Only a dad who can drink expensive wine
Only a dad who cares about everyone
Only a dad who cares about me!

Most people think their dads are the best
Most people say things that come with the rest
But I say something only I can say
I love my dad no matter what they say!

So there you have it all about my dad
He's cool and the best and he's not even a lad
He may be quite old but he's not that bad
So just remember that he's my dad!

Rebecca Ward (12)

# Untitled

You will never ever find
Someone as kind
As my dad
Sometimes when we go out
I'll pick something up
And he'll say no
Because he doesn't have lots of cash
But he always has enough
To throw a big birthday bash
He always has time
To come and play
With me in the day
You will never ever find
Someone as kind
As my dad.

Maddy Hart (10)

# I May Not ...

I may not have a dad,
But my grandad is the best.
He does a lot of things with me,
And asks if I've passed the test.

He takes me out on bike rides,
He takes me through the woods.
When it starts to rain,
We have to put up our hoods.

I really like my grandad,
He is very kind to me.
He asks if I've been good today,
And asks if it's time for tea.

I may not have a dad,
But he's like a dad to me.
He treats me like a princess,
He's one of the family.

Abbie Joslin (10)

# Untitled

My dad is wonderful
He's funny and he's great
I love him very much
For me he's never late

My dad is tall and handsome
I don't mean to boast
But he is
I love him very much
That makes him top of my list!

Rachael Williamson (10)

# Thanks, Dad!

He is a hero,
Meaning the world to me.
He is a tower of strength,
Love, support, security.
He works really hard,
Likes watching sport.
He's my rock, my soul,
The one who inspires me.
My dad shares advice,
Guiding and protecting me.
Helps me through life,
Nine out of ten times right!
He looks after our family,
Stresses, worries - plenty.
Special and unique,
The best dad I could ask for.
He's a treat!
I'd like to thank him in every way,
Finally, I want to say,
No matter how much,
He may moan at me,
He is the only man for me!

Jessica Birch (14)

# Father's Day

**F** irstly a father should be loving and caring
**A** nd always there to help you
**T** he father I love helps me with my homework
**H** earing what I have to do
**E** verybody should love their father
**R** ight now he's playing with me outside
**S** tefano is his name

**D** ad's taken me to the park and I'm playing on the slide
**A** lways happy, I love my father and I just want to say
**Y** eah! It's Father's Day.

Simone Liotti (9)

# A Poem For Dad

Father's Day has finally come,
But I bet your joy's already begun,
Now that your work has all been done,
It's time to sit back and have some fun,
Just leave the work to poor old Mum.

This day is full of love and care,
But the chocolates you will have to share.
I'm going to say this though I shouldn't dare,
To warn you that your head is going bare,
So please really try to grow some hair.

To you this day has been a Godsend,
And I know we'd like more time to spend,
Now that this day is at an end,
But on me you may depend,
Because I'm more than a daughter - I'm your friend.

Lindsay Sivakumar (12)

# A Father's World

*(Dedicated to my special dad who's always stuck by me)*

The sweetest thing is the smile of a father,
The love of one's brother.

The sweetest thing is the eternal bliss of your soulmate,
One that is brought by fate.

The sweetest thing is the morning sun,
The sound of children playing and having fun.

The sweetest thing is knowing you're mine,
A wishing star that will always shine.

The sweetest thing of all is destiny,
Knowing that you and me are meant to be.

*Kanda Ahmed (15)*

# The One, The Only You!

You are a father who is most thoughtful and kind
No matter what the reason
You're there for me each time
With your arms wrapped around me
I feel safe and know you care
Snuggled up against you
Like my cuddly teddy bear
When I'm feeling sad
You readily pick me up
You are like a tonic from an overflowing cup
When things aren't going smoothly
And it's hard to soldier on
Your encouragement drives me forward
And each time I know I've won
So I'd like to say a big *thank you*
For the special dad you are
I'll look up to you always
Because you're my shining star.

Emilie Gust (13)

# My Dad

My dad is fun,
He loves football.
He's a bit tired when he comes home from work,
But he always has time to play with me.
When we play games,
I know sometimes he lets me win.
To me my dad is very special,
Because I love him.
And he loves me,
Even when I'm a bit naughty.
So have a great day, Dad!

*Emma Spicer (8)*

# My Dad

My dad is my own king
He really makes me wanna sing

To guide me through the dark days
Even if we go separate ways

He's my shining star in the sky
He really makes me wanna fly

He'll comfort me with love and care
And is always there for me to share

When I'm hurt he really does care
And when I'm sad he is always there

The future's bright when he's around
He never makes me wanna frown

I love my dad loads and loads
I can't say anymore, I'm gonna explode

So now I've said all I have to say
I will treasure this moment from day to day

*I love you, Dad*
*Happy Father's Day.*

Shannon O'Neill (11)

# Simply The Best

Most dads are good
Most dads are fine
But it don't think there are any dads
Just as good as mine.

A good thing about Dad is
He's always up for a go
No matter what mood he's in
He just never says no.

He plays with us
He takes us for a swim
And I try to show
Just how much I love him.

He's the best dad ever
So, Dad, know this on Father's Day
I love you now
And I will every day.

Michael Jerrett (12)

*Dad Dedications*

# I Love My Dad

I love my dad.
He gets grumpy,
He gets mad,
He gets happy,
He gets sad.
I love my dad.
He's my taxi,
He's my bank,
He's the person
I forgot to thank.
I love my dad.
He's my friend,
He's my enemy,
But when I'm ill
He's my remedy.
I love my dad.
He's there for me,
No matter what,
He's the best dad
Of the lot.

Rebecca Dixon (11)

# Why I Love My Dad So Much

The most important person in my life is my dad
He is always glamorous and glad
And is never, ever sad
No wonder he always cheers me up whenever I feel bad.

Whenever he cracks a funny gag
It might make him look a little mad
But people always say that he is a cheerful lad
And that a good sense of humour he has always had.

My dad is a bit chubby
His nickname would be quite nice as Mr Blobby
But I don't really care
All I know is that his love is always in the air.

*Zaynah Sayed-Ackbar (13)*

# Father's Day!

My dad is cool
My dad is fun
My dad has style
He's number one

My dad has laughs
But sometimes he's sad
My dad is adventurous
So he's not really that bad

My dad is scary
My dad is strange
My dad is a mechanic
I would never want him to change!

There are reasons he is cool
There are reasons he is mad
But all I have always had
Is a really great *dad!*

Maddison Parker (11)

# Daddy

*(Dedicated to Tom Mulholland)*

On this your 13th Father's Day,
I'd like to thank you lots,
For raising me these past 12 years,
Me and the other 4 tots.

Although I have my mother's eyes,
Her hair and face too,
The blood of you flows through me,
And makes me just like you.

It's hard to find a special thing,
But what we have is true,
And what I have to say,
Is father to daughter, me to you.

I'd like to say thank you,
For all the hardship and the tears,
I'm grateful, Daddy,
For all your love over the years.

Brighde Mulholland (12)

# Dream Dad

My dream dad, the one I could ever wish for,
He would love us with all his heart and soul,
He would make us laugh and cry with joy.

My dream dad would be a loving and caring dad,
He would make us a part of his life,
He would gladly give his life for us to make us happy,
He would fill our hearts with love for him.

My dream dad when he dies will go Heaven,
He will be laughing and joking with all the other angels,
All his hopes and dreams would come true,
He will be the best loved angel ever.

This is my dream dad,
It's not just a dream,
But it's reality because this is my dad,
The number one dad, in the world.

Neelam Shahid (13)

# My Dad

My dad is like monkey,
Or are monkeys like my dad?
He always makes me giggle,
When I'm feeling sad!

My dad is like a lion
Watching the sunrise,
He likes to laze around,
Reading about spies.

My dad is like a beaver,
Everything must be the right size,
He's a hard worker,
And very organised!

Katie Wilkinson (12)

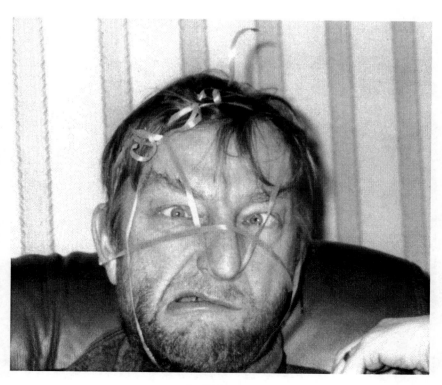

# Guess Who?

He is tall, not small
And he makes me laugh
He is kind, not blind
He is also tough
He is clever, hates leather
He is always fast
He is mad, not bad
And he hates lots of dust
He is busy, never dizzy
And he likes football
He is crazy, not lazy
And he hates being tall.

Guess who?
Yes, it's my dad!

Jessica Meta (10)

YOUNG WRITERS

# For My Dad - John Hickland

My dad is caring,
He's also sharing,
He likes a good game of golf!

My dad has grey hair,
He's also got green eyes,
He doesn't look at all like Rudolph!

My dad is hairy,
He's also very scary,
And he's always very fair!

We are his children,
His mischievous children,
Who always really care!

Maria Hickland (9)

# My Dad

My dad is the best
Better than the rest
He's cheeky as a monkey
His dancing is really funky
He's cool as a cucumber
Is really good with numbers
He's funny as a clown
Never ever frowns
He's clever as a cat
Always wears a hat
He's skinny as a lamp post
And always eats toast
He's busy as a bee
And will always love me.

Kyle Brannagan (10)

# I Love ...

I love my dad,
He's the best thing I have ever had,
He's funny and charming
But his beard is quite alarming!
My dad is a big fan of racing bikes,
F1 racing is what he likes.
I love my dad,
He is the best thing that I could ever have!

Nikki Mawson (11)

# A Poem For Dad

My dad is the best,
No one can beat him.
He is the only one called David M King.

He made our shed and guinea pigs' run,
And also works with computers.
He goes to the Beehive pub,
And sometimes goes to a bar.
If I had to choose a dad
It would be my dad.

Sasha King (8)

# My Dad Robin

**M** y dad Robin is a really great dad,
**Y** es, he is the best I've ever had!

**D** ad is funny, friendly and kind,
**A** nd the best dad you'll ever find!
**D** ad is a super guy.

**R** eally enjoys steak and kidney pie!
**O** h I'm so lucky to have a dad like him,
**B** est dad competitions he does win!
**I** really love my daddy Robin,
**N** o, I can't think where I'd be without him!

*Cathy Comerford (12)*

# Father's Day Poem

Happy Father's Day,
You don't have to pay,
You are the best,
You're warm like a cosy nest.
Happy Father's Day,
Happy Father's Day!
In come the family with the presents,
Some with T-shirts, some with beer,
And even some with chocolates.
All dads are number one,
Just like you, Dad,
Let's play and have fun!

Emma Fielding (9)

# Father, Father

Father, Father, you're so special to me,
That's why I always make your cups of tea.
Father, Father, I don't know what to do,
Because no one is as special as you.

Father, Father, you're the best,
So much better than all the rest.
Father, Father, I love you so,
You're even better than my little toe.

Father, Father, you're like a god to me,
You always hold the golden key.
Father, Father, all I have to say,
Love to you on Father's Day.

Lucy Paige (13)

# My Dad

*(Dedicated to Dad)*

This is a poem about my dad,
When he was growing up he was so bad,
Going off-limits, taking risks,
Biking, getting into fights,
Punching out people's lights,
And oh, how he used to be so menacing,
Jumping over the garden fencing,
Then accidentally running into trees,
And cracking open his skinny knees,
Blood everywhere, a big red mess,
You'd think that would stop him but, oh no, it didn't.
He got *even* worse.
I bet Nan and Grandad thought that they were put under a curse,
He nearly set fire to the garage (trying to show off),
If I knew what was coming I'd go and hide in the loft.
He then got more mature to get a job as a paper boy,
Earning and saving to get a computer game
Or a remote controlled toy.
He met my mum at Granada TV,
They fell in love, got married
And had us three.
I suppose he's not that bad now,
He's not embarrassing,
And his support is everlasting.
Although in youth he was quite bad,
However, he will always be my beloved dad!

Emily Barrett (13)

# Poem For Dad

'Men! Who needs 'em?' we all say
But one man's been here every day
To face the pain, destroy the fear
To wipe away each crystal tear

To draw the lines I mustn't cross
He's strict, don't mess, he *is* the boss
Though he's fair in what he does say
He's the perfect dad, in every way

He understands when things go wrong
Supports me, reassures me, life goes on
Life doesn't always treat you how it's supposed to
But in the end, it brings us closer

He made me who I am today
He's honest, hard-working and brave
I wouldn't say it if it wasn't true
But, Dad, I hope you know
I'll always think the world of you.

Joanna Cawley (14)

# My Dad Paul Moore

You're a twinkle in the eye
Never wears a tie
Out on Friday nights
Near the glowing lights
Always happy all the time
Don't care if he's out
But we are always happy for him
Paul Moore
My dad
A brilliant dad
That's what he is.

Lauren Moore (9)

# A Father Is ...

A father is like a teddy bear
A father is good
A father is crazy
A father is never lazy

A father is a worker
A father is a nurturer
A father is a friend
A father is like a wise owl

A father is a snorer
A father is a footballer
A father is a gardener
A father is a chef.

Sarah Tennick (10)

# A Father Is ...

A father is a grizzly bear
But with a lot of hair
A father is a silly bear
A father is a Billy bear
A father is a careful man
A father is a soggy boggy
A father is a prickly bush
A father is a lovely bugely
A father is a homely lonely
A father is one person that I love.

Emma Nicholson (9)

# A Father Is ...

A father is ...
A cuddly bear
Even though he hasn't much hair.

A father is ...
A person who makes you laugh
Especially when you're in the bath.

A father is ...
Someone who makes you brunch
And the next day buys you lunch.

A father is ...
A loving man
Who's always loving for me
*And that's why my dad's special.*

Matthew O'Toole (10)

Football

What a Special dad.

# Untitled

Sorry, Dad, I didn't think
Sorry, Dad, next time I will put my dishes in the sink
You know, Dad, that it's not that I don't care
It's Mummy's fault - she's never there.

Sorry, Dad, you can repaper the wall
Sorry, Dad, I never meant to let it fall
You do know, Dad, that I love you so much
It's just that Mummy said, 'Please don't touch.'

Sorry, Dad, I will try to be good
Sorry, Dad, I will try to behave as I should
You do know, Dad, that I am only your son
And all I want from life is to have some fun.

David Thomas (11)

# My Dad

My dad is happy, grumpy, sometimes funny
But always there when I am sad
Which makes me feel all so glad

My dad is always sad
When I am bad
But when I am good
He's all so glad

My dad is the best in the world
I wouldn't change him for all the flowers in the wood.

Sophie Marcus (9)

# My Dad

Kind and caring
Loves me to bits
When he gets home
He sleeps and sits

Eyes of blue
Hair is grey
Life's inside
Every day

He's always telling terrible jokes
That he thinks are really funny
He watches TV whilst drinking his whisky
I love him as much as my mummy.

Kate Harwood (10)

# Happy Father's Day

I say happy Father's Day and that makes you so glad.
Today of all days you can't be sad
And of course I won't be bad.
Today I shout hooray
Because it's your special day.
So loving and kind
Even when you have other things on your mind.
You're one in a million
Brilliant without a doubt
That's why I love you so much
And that you need never doubt.
I loved you from the start
And we will never part
And now I say
Happy Father's Day.

Kerry Spence (11)

# My Dad

My dad is really brill
He is very handy with a drill
He is always busy and never still
He doesn't have time to be poorly or ill.

My dad reads to me every night
Making sure that I'm alright
He tucks me in and cuddles me tight
Then he turns off the light.

My dad always finds time to play
Even when it's a horrible, wet day
'I'm in goals,' he will say
But he lets me get my own way.

I have got the world's best dad
He is mine and I am glad
He makes me happy when I am sad
And never tells me off if I am bad!

Megan Nicholson (9)

# Father You Are Dear To Me

Father you are dear to me,
For all you know is to care for me.
Father, you are best as I know,
For you are the most wonderful man.

My father is a king to me,
And I am his princess.
He hugs me every day,
And tells me that he loves me.

My father is the greatest amongst fathers,
My father is never bored.
My father is very bright and loving,
Well, he is all I can afford!

If I were to be Father,
I'd do everything the same.
If I were to lose Father,
It would be the biggest shame.

Father, when you are feeble, old and grey,
I hope I shall reward your care,
For you are so kind to me,
I pray God to spare your life.

Blessing Bakare (10)

# My Dad

My dad, I love so very much,
He's a whiz and kind and fit.
During the summer he plays for a team:
Heysham - cricket.

My dad is only forty-odd,
You wouldn't believe the things he'd do.
I thought running after a ball was a dog's game,
In whites you'd think he'd get flu.

My dad has very dark, black hair,
His eyes are the colour green.
He has the most marvellous temper,
And never is he mean.

My dad works in Fazakerley,
(That's in Liverpool.)
Having to drive there and back in only one day,
He must be a real fool!

My dad, I really love my pap,
Though he is a little odd.
He is always there for me,
So I'm never on my todd.

Peter Townsend (11)

# My Dad

My dad's the best
He's number one
Better than all the rest
Can't be replaced by anyone
But if there's one thing I don't like about my dad
It's that he snores all night like something gone mad
But don't let's ever talk about that now
(Because if we do I might get a row!)
Let's talk about the good things about my dad
Like the way he helps me if I am sad
Or the times he usually buys me sweets
Or presents or videos or loads of treats
He's really kind and helpful
And never, ever fretful
But that's not the reason I love him
I love him because he's my dad.

Laura Foy (9)

# My Dad!

My dad is funny,
My dad is sweet.
My dad is the best,
I repeat.

My dad is handsome,
My dad is kind.
My dad is the one
That makes the sun shine.

Remembering back,
To when I was young.
He would hold me in his arms,
And we would have so much fun.

I never imagined a life so brill,
For my dad makes it special,
So magical and surreal.

Happy birthday, Dad!
You're an amazing person.
I will love you forever,
And we will always be together.

I love my dad,
He's number one.
He's better than all the rest,
Because he's my dad,
*Number one!*

Cassie Culverhouse (12)

# Dad And Me

Dad and me
Sweet as a pea
It's nice to say
You are very special to me!

Dad and me
I love you to bits
I love your wits
It's nice to say
You are the only one for me!

Dad and me
So close we can be
Just you and me
That's the way it's meant to be
Because you are special to me!

*Juliana Matovu (9)*

# My Dad's Cool

My dad's cool
He takes me to school
He takes me to Brownies
And to the swimming pool
He takes me to Scarborough
To see the harbour
We eat fish and chips
And get salt on our lips
He takes me to the fair
On the ghost train there
He takes me to arcades
And buys me buckets and spades
I think my dad's the best
He's better than the rest
But his feet are very smelly
And he's got a big, fat belly
But I love him
He's my dad.

Polly Anna Love (9)

# Poem For Dad

Riches and roses don't mean much to me,
Your love is enough to keep me happy and free.

After a long working day,
You come home to ask me, 'Are you OK?'

I wish you would stop working long hours,
So more time could be ours.

You have always been there for me,
And buy me great things on a shopping spree.

You have always made me comfortable and warm,
Even if you would rather mow the lawn.

You have told me what is right and wrong,
And now I'm thirteen and know how to get along.

I've loved you, Daddy, from the break of dawn,
I've loved you, Daddy, from the day I was born.

Sarah Falkenberg-Hassan (13)

# Daddy

My daddy is a wonder dad;
What can I say about him?
I'll put it in a poem now,
With all my heart and thought in.

**D**   is for darling, my papa he is,
**A**   is for always looking the biz,
**D**   is for daft, his jokes but they're fun,
**D**   is for 'Daddy! The match has begun!' and
**Y**   is for *you,* the best ever dad,

Caring and funny and lovely and mad!

Megan Rose Highcock (12)

# Loving A Dad

I look into the lights of the city
And see your brightness
You reflect into my heart
The same way you make me feel safe
You cover me when I'm down
And let me free
When I am young
You are only that some may say
But you are the light of my life.

Andrew H Pickens (13)

# Papa

Papa, I just wanted to say,
How great you are in every way,
You make my day,
Clearing up all the grey,
Putting a smile on my face,
Us both grinning when we play,
Doing anything and everything just to please me,
You cheer me better than anyone else, you see,
Making me happy all day long,
You are the best father, am I not wrong?
At Manchester United games you have great fun,
Us going to the park in the sun,
Working hard all day,
Listening carefully to whatever I say,
Papa, you are the best,
Much, much better than all the rest,
You should win an award,
Maybe become a lord?
You are just so great,
To decide that we would not need a debate!

Anekha Sokhal (11)

YOUNG WRITERS

# Dad

I look up to this person,
Not only because he is my dad,
But because he is also my friend.
He buys me things and talks to me,
I know I can trust him always,
I love him more than anyone else.
He is my idol,
The great person in my life,
A kind and caring man.
A trustworthy secret-keeper,
A loving family member,
A great comfort to me.
He loves me always,
And I'll always love him.

Angela McDonald (12)

*Dad Dedications*

# My Dad

Fishing crazy,
Shooting mad,
Fixing lorries
That's my dad

Filthy hands
Grease in hair
That's my dad
That one there

Blue-grey eyes
Rough skin
Cuddly bear
That's him

My dad is fun
My dad is cool
My dad is great
The best of them all.

*Caitlin-Jayne Jermey-Thorpe (11)*

# My Dad

My dad has a big belly,
Cos he sits around and watches telly.

He only moves when it's time for bed,
And when he's fully fed.

We've had to have reinforcing in his bed,
Because of the weight from everything he's ate.

He goes to work every day,
And when he comes home we can play.

When it's time to go to bed,
He gives me a hug and kisses me on the head.

Night! Night!

Jasmine May Gray (8)

# My Daddy Is Always There For Me

My daddy wakes me up
And shouts that it is time for school
My daddy gives a goodbye kiss
And a goodbye hug
My daddy is always there for me

My daddy picks me up from school
He asks if I have had a good day
My daddy takes me home and asks me what I want for tea
He said he will make it straight away
My daddy is always there for me

My daddy makes my tea
When Mummy is at work
My daddy looks after me
When I'm ill and I'm off school
My daddy is always there for me

My daddy gives me cuddles
Before I go to bed on a night
My daddy tucks me in
Before I go to sleep
My daddy is always there for me

My daddy will never leave me
Because he loves me
I will never leave him
Because I love him
My daddy is always there for me.

Stephanie Metcalfe

# My Great Dad!

My dad tries to be funny,
But it doesn't really work,
He tells stupid jokes,
Which only makes us smirk,
He does ballet in his underpants,
Which makes him look mad,
He tries to be cool,
Which makes him look really quite sad,
But I love you, Dad, with all my might,
He is always there for me,
Gives me great delight,
I feel quite honoured,
To have such a great and funny dad!
I love you, Dad!

*Brittany Brown (9)*

# My Dad Rules

Although I hardly ever say
My dad's brilliant, super and fantastic in every way
He is like the piece of a puzzle
That makes life just right in my head
I'll know that until I'm dead

He is like the light that guides me through thick and thin
He will never do any sin
He is the person that helps me to keep my head high
At anything bad that happens he won't even sigh

Although this may sound childish, my dad is really fun
And although this may sound lame, his heart could hold a ton
He really is the optimistic type of dad
And although this is quite lame, he will never get mad

In case you haven't noticed from what I have said
I know from my heart and head
My dad really does deserve that teddy bear
He really is the sort of dad that is very rare.

Matthew Kent (11)

# My Dad, My Hero

Dad, you're like a fireman dowsing any heat
Or even a policeman catching robbers at my feet.
You could even be a doctor attending to my cuts.
You're the best a girl could ever have, I love you lots and lots.

You're like a famous wrestler for me to wrestle with
Or even a cool biker for me to ride with.
You could even be a fisherman if I would let you win.
You're a clown to entertain me when I have lost my grin.

Dad, you're always here for me but if you were to go
There are spooks at night so hold me tight and never let me go.
I wouldn't have my playmate or talks just like we do.
I wouldn't have that someone special just like you.

Daddy, you're my hero, I'm as happy as can be.
I've got that someone special to comfort me.
You care for me through thick and thin and never make a frown.
You're all the things a girl would want, you never let me down.

*I love you, Daddy.*

*Georgina Tabberer-Mills (11)*

# Dad To Me (Diamante Poem)

Dad
Big, strong,
Working, laughing, fishing,
Computer, golf, teddy, piano,
Playing, singing, dancing,
Small, cute
Me.

Kelly-Ann Davies (10)

# My Dad

There's a wonderful man who I'm lucky to know,
And day by day he watches me grow.
When I could talk I called him a name,
A name that never lead to shame,
This is a name he has always had,
The name I call him is pronounced *dad!*

When it was bedtime and the lights were off,
I would be scared until I heard *cough, cough.*
That was how I knew my dad was on his way,
He stood in the room and gleamed like it was day.

I wonder how he does it but I don't want to know,
Because it will spoil the surprise when I ask
And he says don't know.

I think he's earned his special day,
To have all things his own way,
Irish football, cricket and darts,
Plus all the love from the bottom of my heart,
Should give him a successful relaxation,
And all the presents he should feel the sensation.

If there was a 'champion dad' trophy awarded,
My dad will win, it's already been sorted,
So if any dads out there would dare to compete,
My dad would still win even if you cheat.

I think that is all I can say now,
Except for happy Father's Day, Dad.

Kirsty Griffin (11)

# Poem For Dad

Dad, this is *not* a poem
On how wonderful you are,
There's a poetry competition and I thought I would enter it.
Sure you can be fantastic, funny
And you deserve a fanfare when you enter the room,
But remember, this is *not* a poem on how wonderful you are.

Yep, this is definitely *not* a poem
On how great you are,
I'm a bit bored so I thought I would write some rubbish,
OK, so you're brilliant, batty and can go seriously bananas,
But should I really write a poem about how great you are?
I think *not!*

Dad, just so you know this is *not* a poem
About how excellent you are,
I mean, it wouldn't even cover half a page!
Yeah, well you can be ace, the alpha, the omega
And rather annoying
But write a poem on how excellent you are? Dream on!

Dad, I suppose this *is* a poem
About how wonderful, great and excellent you are,
After all I have been rabbiting on about you all the time,
Ask my tech teacher,
It's always, 'Dad says this, Dad says that,' during her lesson,
And I suppose I love you very much.

Dad, I'll leave you with three more messages,
1: Please don't ever dye your hair pink again.
2: Don't give your greens to the dog when Mum's not looking,
I'm sure she's getting wise,
And lastly number three would be ...
*Happy Father's Day!*

Polly Brown (13)

# My Dad

I have a secret
For every girl and boy
It's really something special
And nothing you can buy

First thing in the morning
Last thing late at night
A hug is very special
And Dad does it right

When he is at work
I think of him a lot
He's the best dad in the world
He's the only one we've got

He's always at our beck and call
Especially when I fall
He sometimes thinks he's Superman
And stands ten feet tall

Playing games in the house
Outside on the lawn
At the end of the day
Dad will give a yawn

I sometimes think of all kids
Who do not have a dad
To pick you up and hug you
When you're feeling sad

So to all my friends and family
It's something I've been told
Love your dad forever
And be as good as gold.

*Jake Rochfort (10)*

# Poem For Dad

As the day goes along there is me and my family.
My dad is the leader of them all.
The sun shines high in the blue sky.
The water was still and shining.
As we went over to the riverside
My dad's reflection was the only one which shone.
The rest of the family could not be seen.
My dad smiled and the reflection smiled back at him.
The ducks and swans came out to enjoy the light breeze
That was coming across the water.
Then the soft breeze brought an unbelievable surprise.
An enormous black thundercloud was hovering above.
Then for a few minutes the leader was not worried.
Then it was time to worry.
The thundercloud burst.
All of the rain came down and the thunder rumbled.
The leader lead us to the car
And we drove home soaking from head to toe.
The great leader got everybody dry
And in clothes for the rest of the day.
Once again the leader still had the smile upon his face.
This is the dad that will not let you down.
Happy, joyful, smiling father of mine.

*Luke Joseph Nichol (13)*

# Poem For Dad

My dad's the best
But my dad can also be a pest
My dad's number one Dad
Even though sometimes he can go mad.

I love my dad no matter what
I love my dad an awful lot
He can shout and give me a headache
Sometimes I think he can't be a dad, he's a fake.

My dad can sometimes be a pain
But life without him wouldn't be the same
People say when my dad sings it will rain
At least I won't get the blame.

Sky-Jade Walker (11)

# My Dad's The Best By Far

My dad's the best by far,
He's very good on the guitar.

He used to be in a band,
But that was in a different land.

He spends all his time in his studio,
Listening to tunes that I don't know.

He has lots of mates,
They stay till it's late.

He takes them home in the car,
My dad's the best by far!

*Celine Gerrard (8)*

# My Dad - Kennings

Bus driver
Book reader
Snoring sleeper
Football lover
Family carer
Homework helper
DIY doer
Food eater
Dog walker
Laugh maker.

Vicki Good (10)

# My Dad's Groovy

My dad's funny,
Cheery, kind and loving,
He's so patient, never ever running,
But he always rushes to help me when I'm crying.

My dad's the most smashing, tummy tickling,
Sadness riddening, laugh-making person
In the whole wide world.

My dad's a fan of playing games,
Mine a Million and Uno by name,
Football is his number one sport,
To see his team win is his number one thought.

My dad's the most smashing, tummy tickling,
Sadness riddening, laugh-making person
In the whole wide world.

My dad's taught me loads of things ,
He jumps, he dances and he sings,
My dad shows me nearly every movie,
Put this all together and ...
    *My dad's groovy!*

Susan Dowell (10)

# Big Daddy

I like it when you spend time with me,
We can have a laugh and a cup of tea,
And a bacon butty,
Then a game of footie.
You deserve a beer,
And a cheer,
For being the bestest dad,
Even though I drive you mad,
And I'm so lucky to have a dad like you,
Guess what? *I love you!*

Helen Uren (10)

# Dear Old Dad!

My dad arises early at dawn,
Weary and shaven, looking forlorn,
He hugs us, loves us and kisses us too,
He tells us and tells us through and through.
Having a dad so affectionate and kind,
Is really nice but so difficult to find.

My dad washes and cares for his blue Ford Focus,
And when he is doing it he shouts, 'Hocus pocus.'
He looks after and loves my two pet hamsters,
And calls me and my sisters the three young pranksters,
Having a dad so affectionate and kind,
Is really nice but so difficult to find.

We glare at him and we scare him,
And tickle him when he swims,
He takes us on holidays to places where it is hot and sunny,
And everybody in our family thinks he is really funny.
Having a dad so affectionate and kind,
Ain't half great but so rare to find.

We all love him and cherish him,
And to take that off us, well, you wouldn't!

Kimberley Langford (13)

# My Dad

There are many fathers in this world,
They can be good or bad.
But no one could come top of mine,
Cos he's a wonder dad!
Though he may embarrass me,
By dancing down the street,
I really love him very much,
He'll be a hard dad to beat.
His eating habits are rather strange,
Especially when it comes to sauce.
He likes to have it on everything,
Except sprouts of course!
He has many other funny ways,
He worries about going bald.
He counts his hairs each morning,
And asks if he looks old!
I tell him that he doesn't,
And hide a little smile.
That keeps him happy,
Well, at least for a while!
Like most men my father,
Watches the 'beautiful game'.
He supports Plymouth Argyle,
They don't win too often - shame!
I hope this funny poem,
Has summed up the father.
I'm not too bothered about the prize,
It's my dad I'd rather!

*Jenny Barrett (12)*

# Dad

It's hard to find the words to say how much you mean to me,
And how much I love you,
But I'm going to give it a go.

Dad, you are one of the few people that are always there for me,
No matter what,
Despite how horrible I am to you sometimes,
I really don't mean to be.

Day in, day out, you come home after a busy day at work,
Ready to make my tea.
No matter how tired you are always there to help,
And take me places whenever.

When I am feeling really low after a hard day at school,
You are always there with cuddles and kisses,
Ready with something to make me laugh.

When we have our little fights,
We always come out smiling.

You never let me down,
Even though your timekeeping isn't the best.

You are the most caring, kind and the funniest dad ever.
You are one in a million.
I would not change you for the world.

Love you loads, Dad.
Happy Father's Day.

*Claire Dangolitis (15)*

# My Dad

My dad is the greatest
My dad is the best
If you are feeling down
He will cheer you up with his great big smile

My dad likes to eat
Drink a can
Watch the footy match
His team is Man U
If they score a goal
He will run around the room
Pulling his hair out

My dad takes me to my mate's
Whenever he can
Before he has a can
That's my old man

My dad gives me money
My dad is so funny
He is the best dad in the world.

Kerry Blackburn (13)
Beacon Hill School, Aspatria

# My Grandad

My grandad has loads of money
And he thinks he's funny
When others are around
He likes to give me a pound.

When he is at home
He likes to buy a gnome
I think he is the best
Better than all the rest.

When he is at my house
He is as quiet as a mouse
He likes to go to the pub
Or down the rugby club.

John Thompson (12)
Beacon Hill School, Aspatria

# Father's Day Poem

My dad is the best dad
He works at roofing services
At Flimby
He gives me money when I want it

We don't see him much in the morning
All night we do see him
His favourite football team
When he was young was Chester

He likes his gardening very much
He planted tomatoes, sunflowers and potatoes
He loves to have a pint of beer
He loves his liver

He lets me go out when I want
He has a pet called Jack
He called him maniac

He looked after me when I was little
He used to drive a wagon
And I used to go with him
We went to watch the rabbit
When we parked up for the night

He is the *best dad*
Anyone could have.

*Helen Baxter (13)*
Beacon Hill School, Aspatria

# My Old Man

My dad is a farmer,
My dad is the best!
My dad is jolly,
But he can be a wally!

My dad thinks he knows it all,
My dad thinks he's the best.
Sometimes I don't agree with him
When I'm acting a bit dim.

But when he gets a can
He can drink as good as Stan.
Eh! That's my old man.

Liz Atkinson (12)
Beacon Hill School, Aspatria

# My Dad

My good old dad
Port-port
In the sea
On his fishing boat
Sea breeze running through his hair
My good old dad
Giving the bald patch
A good old breeze
Seagulls following
As they go along
Laughing, joking
Through the sea
That's what you call good old dad
1, 2, 3
Man United score a goal
He jumps through the air
With a big, big smile
My good old dad.

*Lee Musgrave (12)*
Beacon Hill School, Aspatria

# My Dad

My old dad
Watches golf on TV
Tiger Woods, that's who he wants to be
And my mum does not approve

My funny dad
He is hilarious
He tickles me till my face goes red
And he is always there for me

My dad's habits are
Always on the PS2
Milking cows
And most of all, golf

My dad likes to watch football
He brings his mates to my house
He drinks and drinks till the match is finished
But he can still fit in some golf

My dad is a character
He is like Homer Simpson
He cracks his jokes
Like an egg.

*Karl Blackburn (13)*
Beacon Hill School, Aspatria

# Father's Day Poem

My dad is so funny
He makes me happy and gives me money.
He keeps me amused all day long
My dad's the best by far bar none.

He is like a cuddly bear
My dad can love and care.
My dad is a wagon driver
My dad is a jiver.

My dad looks after me
He makes me happy as can be.
My dad makes me glad
It's too late, *he's my dad.*

John Strong (12)
Beacon Hill School, Aspatria

# My Dad

I like my dad
He makes me glad,
He helps me when I'm sad
I like my dad.

My dad looks after me all year
He always shows his care,
He can be as scary as a bear
But I know he is there.

I have 1 sister
And 2 bros,
My dad is top class
He is a pro.

Arsenal is his team
To play with them is his dream,
I like my dad
He makes me glad.

Liam Day (13)
Beacon Hill School, Aspatria

# My Dad

My stepdad is the best,
My real dad's in Leeds,
It's for the best.

My dad takes me to footy,
He used to take me to the potty,
He supports the red Scousers,
And I support the white Yorkshires.

He likes the Grand Prix,
He takes my little bro for a pee,
We play football at Crosby,
I always win, he lets me.

Sean Law (13)
Beacon Hill School, Aspatria

# My Daddy

My dad is the best
He's better than all the rest
He is so cool
He is no fool
Because he is just the best.

He gives me money
And he loves honey
He is a cuddly bear
And he really does care
Because he is just the best.

My father takes me places
He is not racist
He buys me nice stuff
And never goes off in a huff
Because he is the best!

Vincent Pierce (13)
Beacon Hill School, Aspatria

# Dad

When I came into the world
You held me in the palm of your hand
My tiny fingers wrapped around your thumb.
How ironic the roles have switched
As a teenager, you are the one
Forced to comply with my demands.

What else are dads for but to be wrapped
Around their daughters' fingers?
So much to give.
Eternal springs of wisdom
Ready to listen to our next trauma or demand.
Knowing exactly the best words to say.

Fathers are a special gift -
Irreplaceable, unique, strong.
My special dad.
Although the waves of life wash over you
Sometimes calm, often tempestuous
Your love for me is constant.

You are there and I am here -
Your words of wisdom echo in my heart.
I will never be without guidance
As I soon fly from the cocoon of security.
Yet you will always be with me
My friend.

Rachel Hamilton (17)
Ballymena Academy, Ballymena

# Daddy!

My daddy is happy,
My daddy is cool.
But sometimes when I'm naughty,
He's strict about the rules!

My daddy drives a car,
It's a Renault Scenic Megane.
Although he will eat anything,
He loves pancakes fresh from the pan!

My daddy is a trendy guy,
He's always up to date,
But sometimes his clothes aren't really nice,
Like his new jacket *I hate!*

My daddy is a loveable chap,
He'd never do anything bad,
He loves our family like crazy,
And he loves me like mad!

*I love my daddy!*

Stacey McGavock (11)
Broughshane Primary School, Broughshane

# Dads

Dads are great, dads are fab
Some use them like a taxi cab!
They're fun, they're loving,
And they make you smile
When you are blue.

So I think without a doubt
That Friday should be their special day;
With breakfast in their bed
And some coffee by their side!

Hugs and kisses all around
To show how much we love them
But I think my dad's the best
Cos he's always there when I need him!
So rock on, dads;
And keep on with the loving!

*Jennifer McCandless (11)*
Broughshane Primary School, Broughshane

# A Loving Heart

My dad, as caring as can be
Although he creeps me out by
Touching horrid things.

He acts a bit like Superman
Without the special powers
But to me he's 'Super Dad'.

With the jokes he tells
He ends in a large laugh and often
It's not the joke, it's the laugh.

And even when it's cold or wet,
He never ever wears his brown coat.

That's my dad!

Simon Paul Dyble (11)
Cottingham

# Dads Are ...

Dads are helpful,
Dads are fab
Because they are around
When you need help from them.

They'll always be there
When you need them the most
Even when you need
To butter the toast.

It's so much fun
Having a dad
He's very helpful at the post office
And at any other job.

He does the shopping
Even though it makes you cheerful.

Dads are so much fun
When they are around
Even if you need help reading
And doing homework.

And they give you a good chance
Of a good treat.

DIY, that's what my dad does, in some of his spare time
Or cutting the grass or cutting trees.

*Happy Father's Day!*

Adam Peckitt (12)
Cottingham High School, Cottingham

# Happy Father's Day

I'm thinking hard
What can I write?
I'll get you a card
But the space is too tight
I need some inspiration
It might cost some dosh
Maybe some information
No, that'll be too posh
I'll write you a poem
I'll write you a book
Yeah, one with mermaids
And Captain Hook
Wait a minute
It'll take too long
I'll just write a paragraph
I can't go wrong
No, no, no, it'll be boring
What can I do?
Maybe we could go touring
In London Zoo
What am I thinking?
I can't afford it
Your smiles and your winking
(Sigh) while I sit there blinking
It has to be special
So what can I do?
I know what ...
This is what I'll say
*Hip hip hooray*
*Happy Father's Day!*

Yasmin Holmes (12)
Cottingham High School, Cottingham

# Mad About Dad

I love my dad
He's never sad
People say he's funny
I say he's mad
He reads my homework
And says that's great
That makes me feel good
He's my best mate
I love my dad
He mends Mum's car
She's so happy
She said he's a star
He plays football
With my little brother
It's great, it's fun
He's like no other
When Mum's at work
He cooks our tea
Yeah, he's done it again
Our favourite spaghetti
As I have told you
I love my dad
And did I tell you
His name is Gav?

*Jordan Palmer (11)*
Cottingham High School, Cottingham

# Footie Mad Dad

My dad is great
My dad is fun
Reading he hates
But loves the sun

He watches TV
All the time
With me and my mum
He is always calm

Football mad
That's what he is
Yes, he's a Chelsea lad
The Blues is the bizz

His fave player is Duff
Yes, number eleven
It's all football stuff
At number seven

For a living he is a gardener
Trees and flowers all the talk
He is always in the garden
With his trowel and fork

Friday night
He is out on the town
Leaving my mum
In her dressing gown

My dad is great
My dad is fun
Football he loves
And adores the sun.

Francesca Gibson (12)
Cottingham High School, Cottingham

# A Special Person

I know a man who is honest and kind,
This sort of man is hard to find.

I know a man who is gentle and caring,
I know a man who believes in sharing.

I know a man, big and strong,
Who tries to show me right from wrong.

I know a man who is clever and bright,
And always there to say goodnight.

I know a man who always knows best,
He's my north and south, my east and west.

Tennis, golf and football we play,
We share a laugh every day.

And the reason why I'm all so glad,
This special person is my *dad!*

James Duncan (12)
Cottingham High School, Cottingham

# A Dad's Poem

My dad's great
The best dad in the world
He may be losing hair
But he's still the best

My dad may be embarrassing
With his bad jokes
And his dancing style
But he's still the best

I love fishing
Just like my dad
He's better than me
Because he's the best

I play football
Just like my dad
He taught me everything
Because he's the best

My dad takes me swimming
In his spare time
My dad's really fun
That's why he's the best.

Aaron Mews (12)
Cottingham High School, Cottingham

# Definitely Dad

My dad is the best although his habits are strange
He likes to watch the history channel ... boring
Or he takes us camping which is great
'Cause I spend time with him.

Your dad's nowhere near as good as mine
My dad lets only me walk my dog
He lets me watch TV when I want
And is simply the best.

Dark chocolate is his favourite
As well as Planet Rock
He likes camping and swimming
He sometimes likes to drink tea.

Although me and my brothers argue
He still loves us, I hope
He gets annoyed when people shout
But who can blame him?

Dad is just the best dad
And I wouldn't trade him for the world.

Phoenix Brown (12)
Cottingham High School, Cottingham

# A Dad's Poem

Oh great, Father's Day is round again
Let's just hope it doesn't rain.
You are so lucky this present you will get
Sit down first though, I would
When you've read this you'll need a vet.

Dad, you are oh so kind to me,
Doing all the cooking, see.
After working all day,
There is something I ought to say,
'Thanks a lot, so just today,
Please have your way.'

You are a dad who's full of fun,
Even though you don't have a son,
Your jokes though are very lame,
Which proves my point, you're quite insane.

Please though, just think of Mum,
Before you release something from your bum!
Please also could you stop snoring?
After a while it does get boring.

Thanks, Dad, for being you,
I'd like you to know I love you too,
Even though you have a hairy chest,
I still think you are the best!

From your 'cheeky, little imp'!

Ruth Bower (12)
Cottingham High School, Cottingham

# Dear Dad ...

Dear Dad, you're the very best,
Dear Dad, you're better than the rest.
Dear Dad, you're fine, just fine,
Dear Dad, you're mine all mine.
Dear Dad, can't you see ...
I love you because you love me!

*Emma Winder (10)*
Crowan Primary School, Camborne

# Father's Day 2005

My dad likes
Tidy handwriting
Reef sandals
Stella Artois and
*Big hugs*

My dad hates
Man United
Me tickling his feet
Grimsby Town FC losing and
Slimy olives

My dad is
A bossy warrant officer
A food lover
A big softie
But most of all
He's my *daddy!*

Emily Masterton (10)
Crowan Primary School, Camborne

# My Dad Isn't Perfect!

My dad isn't rich,
My dad isn't poor,
My dad isn't a giant,
My dad isn't small.
My dad isn't famous,
But my dad is:
A very hard worker,
And he's my dad,
The best dad in the world,
And you can't change my mind!

Kieran Woolcock (11)
Crowan Primary School, Camborne

# Good Old Dad

My dad loves a case of beer
To swap for his hedge trimmer
My dad loves a fish paella
What he'll do for a dog called Stella
My dad loves me

My dad hates those stupid adverts
More than being phoned up at night
My dad hates fatty McDonald's
He'll cover our eyes when we go past
My dad hates the school giving forms
For every time we go somewhere

My dad is a good old doctor
My dad can be silly sometimes
But sometimes he can be serious
But always my good old dad.

Jamie Fairlie (11)
Crowan Primary School, Camborne

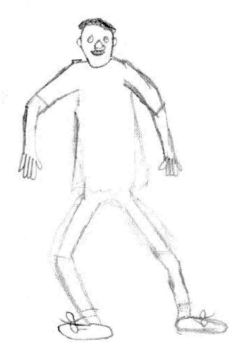

# My Dad Is ...

My dad is who my dad is,
My dad is a great rugby player.
My dad is a great comedian.
My dad is who my dad is.
My dad likes what my dad likes.
My dad likes sleeping in on Sundays.
My dad likes to read a good book.
My dad likes what my dad likes.
My dad hates what my dad hates.
My dad hates a warm beer.
My dad hates noisy buses.
My dad hates what my dad hates.
The only day he gets justice
For all the great things he does is on ...
*Father's Day.*

Paul Fisher (11)
Crowan Primary School, Camborne

# Dads Are Great

Dad, you're great, the best in the world.
Dad, you're mine and you're fine.
I love you so, most in the world -
You're kind, funny, cuddly, caring, sweet -
*Everything*
And you're *mine*
Mine you are forever and ever
Don't go away, not now, nor ever!

Paige Ansell (10)
Crowan Primary School, Camborne

# My Dad!

My dad likes a nice, cold beer,
My dad likes a big, loud cheer.
My dad likes the football team West Ham,
My dad likes a Sunday roast lamb.

My dad hates getting up late,
My dad hates getting up at eight.
My dad hates the tattoos on his arm,
My dad hates the smell of a farm.

My dad is cuddly and round,
My dad is a funny clown.
My dad is always working,
My dad is always burping.

You are the number one, Dad!

*Shennen Barton (11)*
Crowan Primary School, Camborne

# My Dad

My dad likes the smell of farms in the morning
The taste of ice cream
The look of roast and his bed
He hates the fact that
He's out of beer when his birthday's getting near
He hates it when he's bored and sick of the same old channels on TV
He is cool
He's not tall
He's *my dad.*

Joshua Thomas (10)
Crowan Primary School, Camborne

# My Dad

My dad likes Spurs,
My dad likes Tiger Woods.
My dad likes beer,
My dad likes cuddling.

My dad hates germs,
My dad hates losing a bet.
My dad hates fruit,
My dad hates getting told what to do.

My dad is a muscle man,
My dad is a super-duper golfer.
My dad is a wild thing,
My dad is the best dad in the world.

Oliver Hickey (11)
Crowan Primary School, Camborne

# How To Be A Number One Dad

To be the best dad in the world
You'd have to be these things:

Number 1.    Cuddly
Number 2.    Sweet
Number 3.    Lovely
Number 4.    Kind
Number 5.    Bubbly
Number 6.    A shoulder to cry on
Number 7.    Fun
Number 8.    Caring
Number 9.    Cool
Number 10.  You'd have to be *my* dad!

Lily Edwards (10)
Crowan Primary School, Camborne

# My Dad

My dad likes rugby,
My dad likes cricket,
My dad likes beer,
My dad's the best.

My dad hates footballers diving around,
My dad hates rainy days,
My dad hates darts,
My dad's the best.

My dad is brilliant,
My dad is great,
My dad is super superb,
My dad is simply the best.

*Hooray for Dad!*

Tom James (10)
Crowan Primary School, Camborne

# A Rare Gem

Oh Father
A rare gem is what you are
You are very great
You are like a beautiful stone
Which has been cut into a special shape
You are a precious gem
The mightiest man of all men
No one has ever been as great as you
You who fought with hands and feet
To make me survive
Your works are so great
Even kings obey your orders
Father, coin of gold, shining coal.

Truthful one, willing to die for all
Even words cannot tell how I love you
You are dearer to me than the light of my eyes
Dearer than silver and gold.

You are like a cloth which has no stains on it but just white
Many people are searching for you but none have found you, only I
Even trees bend to let you pass
Great Father, king of the Niger
Your eyes are as bright as the light of the sun
But yet wisdom itself you possess
I know of many who kill, I know of many who devour
But you are none of these.

Wrestlers are strong but you are stronger
Your works are great
And your speeches are strong
Oh my dear father
You are a real gem.

Maobong Amos (15)
Demonstration Secondary School, Nigeria

# My Father

My father,
A father most children will desire to have,
Leading you in a path that is always right,
Refusing oppression and wickedness with a passion,
Despising immorality and nudity with an action.

My father,
A disciplinarian,
Never hiding the truth from anyone,
Always sincere,
Easily angered like fire and gas,
Intolerant like the lion but gentle as a dove,
And wise as the serpent;
A loving father.

My father,
Yes, a man but very emotional,
Highly comical and very principled,
Like a hot/cold water so he is uncertain as the weather,
And certain as the seasons but focused as the sharp shooter.

My father,
Forgiving,
Loving, compassionate and caring.
Oh what a father I've got amongst fathers.

*Egwa O'Martha (17)*
Demonstration Secondary School, Nigeria

# A Landmark To The Nation

Who had always been so understanding
His love and care unending and undying
Making me feel loved and unneglected
Even when I was deserted and dejected
Always you, Dad

I always see your care and concern like an unquenching fire
Which burns non-stop to satisfy our needs and desire
You are a man of peace
A man of patience
And a man of endurance

Who never neglected his duty as a father
Always fighting for the welfare of others
Like a master being the slave of his servants and workers
What a good example you led in the sense of duty towards others
Always you, Dad

I will never forget what you did for me
The examples you showed to us I can't mention
For any problem I brought, you had the answers and solution
Always finding time to listen to me
To listen to what I had to say
Indeed you are a landmark to the nation.

*Shatu R Tuki (16)*
Demonstration Secondary School, Nigeria

# Dad

Thank you for all of my toys
You are very funny when you say silly things
When I am sad you make me happy
Dad is special because he always plays with me
He is special because he's funny
He makes me laugh when he can't get the computer on
He is very clumsy when he drops all of his tools
He is always lazy when he doesn't get out of bed.

He is the greatest dad in the world.

Adam Stevens (9)
Drighlington Primary School, Bradford

# My Dad

My dad is special
Because he is funny
And makes me laugh when I'm sad.

My dad is special
Because he takes me places
In the car.

My dad is special
Because he is kind to me!

My dad is special
Because he gives me lots of hugs
Every day of the week.

My dad is special
In every single way
*Hip hip hooray*
I'm glad he's mine!

Lauren Taylor (9)
Drighlington Primary School, Bradford

# My Dad

My dad is special
Because he makes my tea and dinner.

My dad is special
Because he buys me presents and plays games with me.

My dad cheers me up when I am down
By dancing around the room like a clown.

My dad tells me silly stories
Like the runaway train and puts on silly voices
Like he's going insane.

Andrew Bailey (8)
Drighlington Primary School, Bradford

# Dad

Thank you Dad for everything,
you were the one who cared and loved for me.
You set a great example, now I will follow in your footsteps;
you always looked out for me,
anything I wanted you would buy it for me.

Thank you Dad,
when Mum's already asleep, you tuck me in and give me a kiss
but you always do something wrong like forget to close the curtains.
When you come home from work you might have a drink
and if I asked if I could have it, you would say yes.

Thank you Dad for taking me to different places.
If you're going out you always come and ask if I want to come
with you, you always ask how my day has been.
I love you Dad, so much. How could I ever wish for a better dad.

Grace Daji (9)
Drishlington Primary School, Bradford

# Dad

You may be easily persuaded,
But that doesn't bother me.
You drive my mam crazy
Which still doesn't bother me.
Even though I have to make you tea in the morning,
That kind of gets on my nerves.
But when you take me to school in the lorry
That's as cool as cool can be.
You give me DVDs and VCR players all in 1 and build up my bed.
But your singing gets in my head.
When you play games of pool with me down in the pub
And before school I avoid the hug ...

You're still the best dad in the world!

Cain Harniess (9)
Drighlington Primary School, Bradford

# Dad

I think my dad is really funny and daft
Because he went to bed when he was drunk with his clothes on.
I love my dad because he buys me loads of stuff
And he says silly things to me when I'm not feeling well.
I think my dad was brave
When he got the Land Rover stuck at Leeds/Bradford airport.
My dad is special to me
Because he takes me everywhere with him.
My dad is the best.

Jodie Mitchell (9)
Drighlington Primary School, Bradford

# Dad

My dad is special in lots of ways
Because he takes me on holiday and fun parks every day.
My dad once went on a pogo stick and fell off
Because he's insane and he was in a lot of pain.
Every time I look glum he comes and cheers me up
And we have lots of fun.
My dad is kind and cheerful
And when I am stuck and can't do something
He always comes and helps me.
When I'm doing sports day my dad cheers me on.
He is my number one!

Lucy Solomons (8)
Drishlington Primary School, Bradford

# My Dad

My dad has got a motorbike
He's not the sort who will hike.
I love my dad lots and lots
Even though he makes me wash the pans and pots.

My dad goes to work to get us money
And when he's at home he's funny.
I love my dad a lot.

Leanne Margison
Gawthorpe High School, Padiham

# Untitled

Here he goes again,
Winding me up once more!
If he carries on,
I'll go and slam the door!

But I love him to pieces,
I'm glad he's my dad!
He makes me good cheeseburgers,
They're really, really fab!

Naomi Moore (13)
Gawthorpe High School, Padiham

# My Super Dad

My dad is the best
He's better than the rest.
All the rest really drool
Mine's the best, he's really cool.
When he's away I know he's not far
He'll come and collect me in his top car.
When we fall out I know it's not bad
Because he is a top super dad.
My dad is the top
He got chased by a cop.
I thought it was funny
My dad got me a bunny.
He's got the money
So he buys me stuff.
I love my dad
He's the top dad ever.

Rebekkah Davies
Gawthorpe High School, Padiham

# Untitled

Through good times and bad
Happy times and sad
There's one person I can rely
He'll always try
That's my dad.

Through night and day
He'll keep my demons at bay
By my side he will be
His love for all to see
No one can take that away

Have fun and argue like mad
When I'm down he makes me glad
If I'm sad and start to cry
He'll make me feel I can fly
That's my dad.

Emma Foden (13)
Gawthorpe High School, Padiham

# Dad's Been In The Bathroom Again!

Aftershave everywhere
Towels on the floor
Bathroom's all messy
Dad's been here once more.

You're a perfect example
For a perfect dad
You're mostly sound
But rarely mad.

I love you so much
You're the best in the world
With my mum as you're wife
And your three beautiful girls.

Katy Barsby (13)
Gawthorpe High School, Padiham

# My Footy Mad Dad

I love my dad
He is footy mad,
He loves me too
Even when I'm bad.
He is good to me
He helps me all the time,
I am so glad
That he is mine.
I'm writing this poem
Just to say,
You deserve a happy
Father's Day.

Kayleigh Norcross (12)
Gawthorpe High School, Padiham

# Untitled

At the end of the night
When I shut my eyes tight
You are always there

My stepdad you may be
But happy are we
That you are always there

Sometimes I'm bad
But whenever I'm sad
I know you are always there

I know I'm a pain
Drive you insane
Guess what? You're still there

Always around
Always to be found
Our family you've made complete
But however hard you try
Mum's cooking you'll never beat!

Josh Cochrane (13)
Gawthorpe High School, Padiham

# A Dad Should Be ...

A dad should be kind,
And a dad should be selfless,
A dad should be wise,
And a dad should be helpful,
A dad should be cool,
And a dad should be strong,
But most of all a dad should be there,
To give happy memories of love,
And of care.

*Matthew Fletcher (13)*
Gawthorpe High School, Padiham

# Untitled

I've got a dad who lives away,
I go to his house every Wednesday,
My dad is mad, a silly fool,
But he's the best, he's really cool.
He buys me clothes, CDs and candy,
He loves to drink, especially brandy.
He takes care of me when I'm ill and sad,
He really is a super dad!

Charlotte Jaggers
Gawthorpe High School, Padiham

# My Dad

My dad's not enthusiastic,
He doesn't fly spaceships to the moon,
Drive fast cars round all day,
Balance a ball on a spoon.

My dad's not that wild,
He doesn't roller-skate in the park,
Disco diva till he drops,
Trick or treat in the dark.

He is just there,
He cares,
That's all I want for me.

Jade Burnett (13)
Gawthorpe High School, Padiham

# World's Greatest Dad

My dad is great
He is my best mate
He is loving and caring
Gentle and sharing
We do everything together
In all sorts of weather
I love my dad
He is sound
Even though
He's big and round
Love comes in all shapes and sizes
I love him because he gives me surprises
My dad is the best
Better than all the rest.

Chloe Knowles (13)
Gawthorpe High School, Padiham

# Untitled

Mr Moorhouse, Mr Moorhouse,
First name Wayne,
First name Wayne,
He supports Burnley,
He has supported them firmly,
For over thirty years,
He still hears the chanting in his ears.
Mr Moorhouse, Mr Moorhouse,
First name Wayne,
First name Wayne,
He even has a claret car
To follow the trend,
His love for Burnley
Will never end.

Danny Moorhouse (12)
Gawthorpe High School, Padiham

# Super Dad

Super dad must be your name -
Because you're a hero in my eyes.
If there was an award for the world's best dad -
You would win the prize.

You must have special powers -
For all the jobs you do.
You look after our family,
Whatever we might do.

And you must be a genius -
Because you're always there -
To help with my homework
And show me that you care.

And you must be a fab dad -
For just being who you are.
You're all these things and so much more
You're a super dad by far!

Lucy Zirins (13)
Gawthorpe High School, Padiham

# My Dad

My dad likes football
But he hates going shopping
He loves his back garden
But feels sad when it dies
He's just the best dad in the world.

My dad likes to pinch me and sometimes it hurts
He always pumps which annoys my mum
But best of all he all tickles me and makes me laugh
Also he's lazy and takes over the TV
He's still just the best dad in the world.

My dad is the funniest guy in the country
He makes me laugh every day
He's kind and buys me lots of things
Like clothes, toys and sweets
He's just the best dad in the world.

I know my dad shouts a little bit
But I don't care one bit
I know he loves me so, so much
And guess what? I love him too
He's just the best dad in the world.

Jessica Heap (9)
Grosvenor Road Primary School, Swinton

# My Dad Is Cool

**M** y dad is cool because he swims in a pool.
**Y** ou are the best dad in the world.

**D** ad is cool because he is no fool.
**A** t Blackpool he is always funny.
**D** ad is the best and I know he always will be.

**I** s my dad a fool or is he cool?
**S** ometimes my dad is cool but sometimes a fool.

**C** ool dad is a fool and he'll always be one too.
**O** h my dad loves football so much.
**O** ut in the garden my dad acts so cool.
**L** ocked up in the house when we go out.

*Chloe Bowker (9)*
Grosvenor Road Primary School, Swinton

# My Dad

**T** he best dad in the galaxy!
**H** e loves technology
**E** xcept when the computer does not work.

**B** ut he always fixes it.
**E** xcellent he is.
**S** o I think he is very smart.
**T** echnology he loves the most.

**D** ad takes me out anywhere I like.
**A** t the park or even a fairground.
**D** ad loves me so much.

**I** n a way I dislike him for smoking
**N** ot that I hate him though.

**T** he best dad in the galaxy.
**H** e is very nice to me.
**E** ven if I do things wrong.

**W** e all love him.
**H** e loves us too.
**O** f course he is the best to me.
**L** ove him I do
**E** ven if he does smoke.

**W** hen I'm in the park he'll play with me.
**I** love him so much.
**'D** ad', I shout when I need help
**E** ven if I'm only a little stuck.

**G** enerous he is.
**A** t his eyes you'll see a twinkle in them.
**L** ate he is when he is visiting me.
**A** t the cinema he buys me a drink.
**X** -rays he has had on his leg.
**Y** ou wouldn't want to sell him for a thousand pounds.

*Connor Day (9)*
Grosvenor Road Primary School, Swinton

# My Dad

My dad's at work all of the time,
I don't know how he gets his sleep.
He takes us to parks and places
In his huge, shiny jeep.

My dad is the best,
My dad is the best.
My dad is the best,
Even if he thinks I'm a pest.

My dad never fails,
He always cheers you up when you're down.
He never leaves you alone,
He sometimes turns your smile into a frown.

My dad is the best,
My dad is the best.
My dad is the best,
Even if he wears a sweaty vest.

I love my dad a lot,
He is in the right place at the right time.
He is just the best,
Don't you wish your dad was like mine?

Hazel Hilditch (9)
Grosvenor Road Primary School, Swinton

# My Dad

I love my dad
He's really funny
But best of all
He gives me money

My dad makes songs
Up for me
He calls me names
And laughs, hee, hee

I love my dad
He's really funny
But best of all
He gives me money

If I look at something in the shop
He buys it for me
My mum says I'm spoilt
I say good

I love my dad
He's really funny
But best of all
He gives me money

So what I'm trying to say is,
I love my dad,
He's great, he's funny,
He's my dad.

Elspeth Wrigley (9)
Grosvenor Road Primary School, Swinton

*Dad Dedications*

# The Man From Whitchurch!

There's a man in Whitchurch, that's my dad,
He's big and fat, a bit of a lad,
I like it when you make me cheer
So here's a treat, have a beer,
So add together great and kind
And that equals my *dad!*

Steph McCann (12)
Hartcliffe Engineering Community College, Hartcliffe

# To My Daddy, You Know I Love You So

To my daddy, you know I love you so ...
But normally I use you to get a lot of dough
I never want to lose you cos my money will never grow
But if you stay your money will become low.

You took care of me when my face never glowed
I just want to say,
'Are you going to buy me another box of chocolates today?'

You make me laugh, you make me cry
You take me out when the weather's dry.

Your jokes may be bad but you never make me sad
I just want to say happy Father's Day!

To my daddy, you know I love you so ...

Emma-Jade Kingdon (12)
Hartcliffe Engineering Community College, Hartcliffe

# Dad

Dad, you have told me a lot,
Ever since I was in a cot,
You've helped me out when things were bad,
You're the one and only greatest dad.

Dad, I think you're hard as nails,
Because of all your punch up tales,
But I think you're holding back,
The often times you got a smack!

You taught me rugby, rain or shine,
All worthwhile, the trophy is mine,
You got me through all the stages
And - *wow, Dad* - you've had that haircut for ages!

Dad, you met the greatest mum
Then I ended up in her tum.
Couldn't say it then but would like to say
You are the greatest dad any day.

Thanks for everything.

Darren Marshall (12)
Hartcliffe Engineering Community College, Hartcliffe

# Untitled

Dad, you have always been there for me!
I just want to say you're the best dad on Earth.
You have been there ever since my birth.

Dad, we do loads of things together
We do more nice things in hotter weather.

Dad, we'll do great things whenever
I hope we will be like this forever.

Dad, I can't say any more about you
Because there are no words to describe you
No words like great and special
Just you are great and parental
Love you loads.

*Chereale Cormack (12)*
Hartcliffe Engineering Community College, Hartcliffe

# Dad, You're The Greatest

Dad, you give me good advice
You are far more than nice
You hug me when I'm sad
And make me really glad
You support the greatest team
When we watch them we always beam
You watch me play football rain or shine
You shout good stuff all the time
You married the greatest mum
You put me in her tum
When I came I could see
You were the greatest and only dad for me
Dad, you're the greatest
I like being called Davis
Dad, I love you with all my heart
But please, please do not fart
You have a beer belly
But you hope to watch me on telly.

You're the greatest dad in the world
Thanks for the pressies and everything.

Ryan Davis (12)
Hartcliffe Engineering Community College, Hartcliffe

# Grandad

**G** randad, I love you very much
**R** eady and raring to go
**A** nger isn't a good thing, that's why I love you so
**N** ever leave me on my own
**D** ad isn't always there but you are standing ready
**A** nd that's why I care
**D** on't forget that I love you but I don't mind to share!

Michaela Vowles (12)
Hartcliffe Engineering Community College, Hartcliffe

# My Dad

My dad is the best
My dad is one in a million
He looks out for me
And cares for me
My dad is the best
Well, after all he is my dad.

Ellie Burns
Hartside Primary School, Crook

# My Dad

The great thing about my dad
Is he makes me laugh
When I am upset.

The fantastic thing about my dad
Is that he will always buy me
What I want.

The brilliant thing about my dad
Is he reads me bedtime stories
When I go to bed.

But the best thing about my dad
Is that he is the best dad ever.

Hannah Blakey (8)
Hartside Primary School, Crook

# Edwin

**E** xcellent is my dad!
**D** eserves lots of love!
**W** ould win best dad of the year!
**I** ntelligent and caring!
**N** ot for sale, all mine!

Jonathan Page (9)
Hartside Primary School, Crook

# My Dad

**M** agnificent dad
**Y** ou can rely on him

**D** oes his bit to help
**A** lways cares
**D** oes his job to help around

**I** ntelligent man
**S** uper him

**S** o special
**U** nder machines
**P** leasant guy
**E** very day he treats me kind
**R** usty machines he works under.

Jacob Craig (9)
Hartside Primary School, Crook

# Without My Dad

Some children in other countries don't have a dad,
I would be really sad,
Without my dad,
But since he is with me, I am really glad.

Some children in other countries don't have a house,
I would feel like a louse,
Without my house,
I may as well be a mouse.

Some children in other countries don't have clothes,
I would feel like a dead rose,
Without my clothes,
Without my clothes, who knows?

Some children in other countries don't have shoes,
I would get the flu's,
Without my shoes,
I feel like people would give me boos.

I am glad I am a child,
In England,
With a dad,
With a house,
With clothes and
With shoes.

Megan Bryden (9)
Hartside Primary School, Crook

# Father's Day

Now it is Father's Day,
   I just came to say,
   Happy Father's Day,
   So hip hip hooray.

So now it's Father's Day,
   And I'd like to share,
   Just how much I love you,
   And how much I care.

So Father's Day is here,
   So let's all hear,
   For a special dad,
   One loud, big cheer.

Natalie Hopper (9)
Hartside Primary School, Crook

# About Dads

Dads are funny,
And football mad,
They're always smiling,
Like the Cheshire cat.

They're encouraging and helpful,
They have beer bellies too,
They're always there,
Standing up for you.

Some are hardworking,
Others watch TV,
But all of them are there,
To be with you or me!

Natalie Dugdale (11)
Hazelwick School, Crawley

# My Dad Says ...

My dad says eat your greens,
He always says it when he is mean.
My dad says eat your veg,
I just chuck them over the window ledge.
My dad says peas are good,
I think I would ban them if I could.
I hate my dad when he is mean,
Especially when he tells me to eat my greens.

Yasra Rafiq (12)
Hazelwick School, Crawley

# My Dad

My dad is as hairy as a llama,
My dad is as thick as a banana,
My dad smells like a rotten egg,
My dad is as bald as a golden peg,
My dad is as strong as a baboon,
And always eats his food with a spoon,
My dad is always on time,
And drinks the finest of wine.

My dad is fat and lazy,
And always drives me crazy,
My dad thinks he owns the throne,
My dad feels alone.

But I still love my dad,
Even though he drives me mad.

Daniel Jeffryes (12) & Tyler Homeyard (11)
Hazelwick School, Crawley

# My Loving Father ...

He's so good and true.
Although when he shouted I gave him two.
He sits on the couch drinking beer,
However I have a fear.
As time goes past,
He may not be here.
At every second I wish to be with him,
And so does my brother Tim.
As he watches TV wasting his time,
I'd rather prefer he did a crime.
He leaves home saying he's going for some work,
As soon as I tell him I need help with my homework.
He leaves for the office after a cup of tea,
And then he realises he's forgotten his car keys.
But I love him so much.

Katherine Williams & Sundeep Sarai (12)
Hazelwick School, Crawley

# Dad's Personality

Many people have different ideas about my dad,
This is a personal thought that I have always had,
He's supposedly cuddly and kind,
But there is a different side of him to find.

When he's angry he goes bright red,
You really can't bear to look at his head,
His eyes start popping out,
Then he starts to really shout.

Uh oh! I'm in trouble now,
I've got to get out of this but how?
Then he suddenly calms down,
And I can't see his scary frown.

Thank God for that, I was petrified,
It's good he stopped, I could have nearly cried,
But usually he is nice to me,
Which many people often see.

Erin Irwin (12)
Hazelwick School, Crawley

# Dad

Dads are dads and mums are mums,
But all my dad does is twiddle his thumbs,
My mum nags Dad to do DIY,
But he never lifts a finger he would rather die.

He is always very cuddly and warm,
Except when he is filling out a form,
He shouts and screams, he hates the things,
But when he starts to calm down he sings.

My dad has lots of nice things to say,
He says I am brilliant in every way,
He calls me sugar lump and treacle tart,
And sometimes calls me extremely smart.

I love my dad and my dad loves me,
And most people can usually see,
That dads are special in every way,
My dad is the hero of the day.

*Fern Fisher (11)*
Hazelwick School, Crawley

# Poem For Dad

Some are big, some are small,
But you're the best dad of them all.

Your farts smell,
Like I'm in Hell.

You're fun and great,
You're my best mate.

You give me money all the time,
You make my life shine.

When I was little I was scared a lot,
But you were right next to my cot.

People say you're lazy and old,
But I think you're really bold.

You wear crazy things but I don't care,
Because of your wacky, cool hair.

Some are big, some are small
But you're the best dad of them all.

James Jeffryes & Alex Taylor (12)
Hazelwick School, Crawley

# The Perfect Life Of A Dad

He gets up at the crack of dawn
He even has time to mow the lawn.
He goes to work at nine o'clock
When he gets there he's in a bit of a shock.
His kitchen is near to death
But he doesn't want to lose his job as a chef.
He comes home and starts to lay
As it has been a hard-working day.

He gets up at 7 o'clock to cook us a splendid dinner
As he has been our number one winner.
We let him treat himself for a night out with a few mates
Then he comes back very late.

Then it's time for another perfect day.

*Ryan Banton (12)*
Hazelwick School, Crawley

# My Dad!

He's big, fat, bald and lazy
And he nags me all the time,
He's always rather crazy
When he's drunk on his red wine!

He's embarrassing when I'm with my friends
He pulls me off the phone
The things he breaks he never mends
He thinks his chair's his throne!

He makes me do such stupid chores
He doesn't even pay
Being with him is such a bore
He makes me slave away!

He snores so very loud
He wakes me up next door
And after that he acts so proud
Because it shakes the floor!

He gobbles up all the food
There's nothing left to spare
He's gross, disgusting and he's rude
When he eats I wish I wasn't there!

He sings so loud, so out of tune
Especially when I'm on the phone
My friends all think he's a total loon
I hate living in this home!

You must think I really hate my dad
But you couldn't be more wrong
In fact I am truly glad
I've known him for this long!

Hannah Gilbert (11) & Flossie Joseph (12)
Hazelwick School, Crawley

# Poem For Dad

Dad, thanks for everything you've got me
And all those cups of tea you've made me.
The BBQ's were top
Apart from when they had to stop.
The bouncy slide was the best
It was better than all the rest.
Thanks for taking me to Tesco
I thought it was the best though.
All the food was great
Especially on the plate.
Thanks for taking me to Littlehampton
Except for that crab you accidentally stamped on.
I loved all those fish and chips
And looking at all those ships.
Thanks for both my motorbikes
They were a lot better than my pushbikes.
Now I have come to the end
And this is what I send.

*Ryan Towner (12)*
Hazelwick School, Crawley

# Thank You

Daddy
From the day I was born
You have guided my footsteps
Dad
From the day I was born
You have loved me unconditionally
Father
To the day I die I know
I will always be your daughter

Daddy
You made me laugh when I was sad
Dad
You have kept me going where I would have stopped
Father
You have loved me when others would not

Daddy
You inspire me to do better
Dad
Your pride in me has stopped teacher's criticisms from hurting
Father
The stubbornness you passed on to me
Has caused more than one fight
But through it all you have been a guiding light
In a dark world full of madness
Thank you.

Charlotte O'Rourke (14)
Hazelwick School, Crawley

# My Dad

My dad is great,
He gives me money,
He takes me to football,
And he will play with me.

When I play football,
He will encourage me,
It sounds like he is moaning,
But he is telling me what to do.

My dad will do anything,
Play, fight
Or play football to help me
And I will always have fun!

He congratulates me on school,
Also on the football pitch
That is why
I love my dad.

*Kenny Marsh (13)*
Hazelwick School, Crawley

# Dad Poem

Dad is great
He's just like a mate
He likes Jelly Babies
And Wine Gums he hates

Dad is very tall
He loves playing football
Dad is fat
He really hates cats

Dad loves to run
He thinks he's number one
Dad is smart
He loves go-karts

He's a fan of Crystal Palace
So is my auntie Alice
Not only is he my mate
I think he's great.

Ben Howes (13)
Hazelwick School, Crawley

# Dad

My dad has a beer belly,
Loves watching 'Top Gear' on the telly.
He has a 348 Ferrari,
He's mad and is scary like the safari.
He's always spending money on cars,
In other terms he loves nice cars as hot as Mars.
He has four fast cars,
The only sport that he's interested in is sports with cars.
He's always spoiling me,
And he has 1 sugar in his cuppa tea.
He is 38 years old,
When he tells us to do something we jump up
And do as we have been told.
My dad is a great dad.

Adele Stuchbury (13)
Hazelwick School, Crawley

# Poem For Dad

Once while having tea
My dad told me
That he could see
A big, fat humming bee.

My face went red
I couldn't go to bed
Next morning when I awoke
My dad told me it was all a joke.

My dad loves to scare me
Even while having tea.

My dad is very strong
And I am sure he's never wrong
When we argue for so long
It's me who's always wrong.

My dad is very nice
He has never spoken lies
My dad is sweet and wise
And he has got beautiful eyes.

Thank you for everything, Dad
I am so glad
Because you are the best
Better than the rest.

Sanober Vohra (12)
Hazelwick School, Crawley

# Untitled

Number one, number one
My dad is number one
He is always there for me when I'm sad
He calls me a monkey and says I'm mad
Number one, number one
My dad is number one
He's really funny, he's really nice
He tells me off but never twice
Number one, number one
My dad is number one.

Sana Ghafoor (13)
Hazelwick School, Crawley

# Dad

He drives Mum up the wall,
And he doesn't give a damn, not at all,
He would rather go and kick a ball.

He tries to be cool,
But he looks like a fool,
He can't sing,
Neither can he bling,
And he certainly looks like a bit of a ming.

But when it comes to football,
Blue is the colour,
Football is the game,
Chelsea are playing,
Oh! What a shame!

He's football mad,
As you might have guessed,
But he definitely is the very best.

*Bernice Broom*
Hazelwick School, Crawley

# My Dad's Better

'My dad's a taxi driver.'
'Well, my dad's a bus driver.'
'My dad's a beer monster.'
'Well, dad's a fact monster.'
'My dad's got me an Action Man.'
'Well, my dad's got me a big toy van.'
'My dad's bald.'
'Well, my dad's tall.'
'Your dad wears glasses.'
'Well, your dad fails in all his classes.'
'My dad's funny.'
'Well, my dad took me to see Selsey Bunny.'
'My dad's a super Spurs supporter.'
'Well, my dad knows P Diddy's daughter.'
'My dad gets me what I wish.'
'Okay, you win, I'm going to feed my fish!'

Lauren Murphy (13)
Hazelwick School, Crawley

# Special Dad

The special dad is fun,
He can make burgers with two soft buns.

The special dad does not go to a bar,
Instead he works on his car.

He is also smart but not good at art,
That way I think he is stubborn as a cart.

A special dad is great,
And he is never ever late.

He can sing along with every song,
And that is why he is great.

That special dad is lazy,
And his wife thinks he is lovingly crazy.

That special dad,
Is my own dad.

Gowtham Thevarajah (13)
Hazelwick School, Crawley

# Dad

My dad is so great
He puts my dinner on my plate.
My dad is so cool
He drives me all the way to school.
My daddy is so funny
He makes me laugh when he dresses up like a bunny.
My daddy will never make me cry
And if he did he would rather die!
My dad is so nice
He cooks the dinner but burns the rice.
My daddy is so weird
He wanted me to grow a beard.
If I ever get in trouble at school
He'll say, 'Oh well,' and watch football.
My dad is the best ever!

*Jack Thompson (13)*
Hazelwick School, Crawley

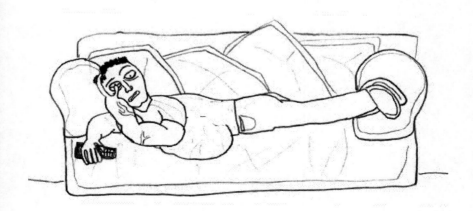

# Dads

Dads, father, daddy,
They give you money.
If you're down and lonely,
They will be sure to keep you groovy.

Dads, father, daddy,
With their big beer belly,
They will be sure to give you honesty
Because this is the best policy.

Natasha Delgado (13)
Hazelwick School, Crawley

# My Dad

My dad is very, very mad,
When he was young he was a bit of a lad.

He takes time to look after me and put me first,
Although when it comes to football, football will come first.

My dad is very, very mad,
When he was young he was a bit of a lad.

He really, really can drive his car just with music on loud,
So loud that it makes your ears go really quiet as a cloud.

He comes round at half-past seven
And we will stay up until half-past eleven.

My dad is the best of the best
And he is better than all the rest.

The more he does the more I love my great old dad
Better than all the rest.

My dad is very, very mad,
When he was young he was a bit of a lad.

'Dad, Dad,' my sister will cry
And will really cry,
'Coming,' I will say but it's all a lie
Because Dad is already here.
He is my dad, all mine.

Domonic Pound (13)
Hazelwick School, Crawley

# My Dad

Some dads are loving,
And some are really boring,
But my dad is lazy and sarcastic.
He goes out at eight and comes back at three.
There was one time he said he'd run away
And drown himself in the sea.
He makes out he's really strong,
Even though he's 4ft 1.
My dad's embarrassing,
People laugh at him every day.
He sunk into some quicksand,
And got his head stuck in clay!

Jasmine Coombes (13)
Hazelwick School, Crawley

# Dads

Some are small, some are tall
And some are in the middle

Some are tubby, some are skinny
And some are in the middle

Some are as loving as Cupid
Some are as loving as the Devil
And some are in the middle

Some are as kind as God
Some are as kind as Satan
And some are in the middle

Some of them are popular
Some of them are not
And some are in the middle

Some of them are dangerous
Some of them are not
And some are in the middle

Some of them drink
Some of them don't
And some are in the middle

But my dad is loving
And everything I want him to be
My dad is my dad
And that's what I want him to be.

*Lauren Hubbard (13)*
Hazelwick School, Crawley

# Dad (Haiku)

He is really great
We sat down by the fireplace
I really miss him.

Lauren Griffiths (9)
Heronsgate School, Milton Keynes

# Dad's Day (Haiku)

It's Father's Day, Dad!
You are a very nice man.
And I love you too.

Emily Siggers (8)
Heronsgate School, Milton Keynes

# My Dad (Haiku)

My dad has green eyes
And he works for Kwik-Fit-Fleet
And is lots of fun.

Natalia Mortlock (9)
Heronsgate School, Milton Keynes

# Dad (Haiku)

I love my dad lots
He is fun, smart and clever
I love you so much.

Laura Willingham (9)
Heronsgate School, Milton Keynes

# My Dad (Haiku)

Good-looking and nice
He likes to play some football
He's a mystery.

Jonathan Venus (8)
Heronsgate School, Milton Keynes

# My Dad (Haiku)

My dad is crazy
My dad is embarrassing
He watches football.

**Kate Mintern (8)**
Heronsgate School, Milton Keynes

# My Dad

My dad is the greatest
He really makes me laugh.
He's good at sport
And when he wins I say,
'That's my dad, yes he is,
He's the greatest dad on Earth.'

Oliver Dean (9)
Heronsgate School, Milton Keynes

# My Dad

When you come to me at night
It gives me quite a fright
I love the teddy
I called it Freddy
I think your chin is
Spiky and thin
You are mad but not sad
When you smile it's in your eyes
Like stars in the sky
You do shout as loud as mighty
You are strange
You crack a joke
And you always laugh at them all
I love you, you love me
That's what it means.

Amber Allcock (10)
Linton-on-Ouse Primary School, York

# Dad

Dad's my
Hero,
Mess-ups
Zero
He scored
Ten goals
And likes
Cheese rolls
My dad
Likes yellow
He's a
Good fellow
Makes stuff
With glue
Polystyrene
Stones too!
He plays
With me
Quick break
Cup of tea
Dad's cool
Dad's great
Can't be
Replaced!

David Garner (10)
Linton-on-Ouse Primary School, York

# My Dad The Greatest

My dad, he's loving, caring and affectionate
And loves me dearly
When I'm with him I feel secure,
And somewhere I'm most wanted
My dad stays in my heart
And when I see him my heart races
With joy and excitement.

My dad is tall and handsome
And feels for others before himself
He likes to explore the world
And find out new things.

My dad has a *huge* heart
But uses it with care
My dad has a deep voice
Deeper than you could ever go
His face will sweat up
And will cry with tears of happiness
Like a cloud ready to start raining.

My dad doesn't live with me
So every time I see him
I always make sure I tell him
'I love you'
Because at the end of the day he's my dad
And that's all I want him to be.

Amy Cawley (9)
Linton-on-Ouse Primary School, York

# Untitled

**D** ad, I know you love me
**A** nd I know how much you care
**D** ad, I know you wish you were always here
**D** ad, I know you want me to have the best
**Y** ou're kind and generous and I know you'll always be there
**S** till you see me as a baby

**L** aughing and joking in the sun
**I** 'll always remember the fun times we had
**T** alking about football ... we're so sad!
**T** offee and cake you love to eat
**L** ots of chocolate is your special treat
**E** nergetic you are definitely not!

**G** rumpy and moody you certainly are!
**I** still am your number one daughter
**R** uth
**L** ove, daddy's little girl.

*Ruth McFarlane (14)*
Lomond School, Helensburgh

# Dad

Dad, you brought me up,
With all your love and care,
Whenever you were needed,
You were already there.

I don't know how I'd have turned out,
Without you at my side.
Because my life, growing up with you,
Has been a crazy ride.

I remember in the kitchen once,
You're cooking was so dire.
You couldn't even boil an egg,
And set the house on fire.

Do you remember when I was teething,
With the ring I used to gnaw?
You came over to the armchair,
And I kicked you in the jaw.

So we've had our time together,
Most of which has been a laugh.
And in my time of trouble,
You have shown me the path.

And on the odd occasion,
When I have caused you pain,
You've forgiven me and you've also said,
'Try not to do it again.'

So now I am no longer small,
Not as childish or as wild,
But no matter what will happen,
I'll always be your child.

Gary McGinley
Lomond School, Helensburgh

# Missing My Daddy!

You used to cuddle me when I was small,
But now I've grown tall,
You helped me out whenever I fell,
But now I always seem to be well,
You comforted me when I was upset,
But now all I seem to do is regret,
How little time I've really spent with you,
I really miss you, Daddy.

Now you live far, far away,
But I wish you'd live here with me today,
All I can do is call you on the weekend,
Or even write a letter that I would send,
It feels so alone,
To not have you here at home,
I wish I could see you every day, Daddy.

I just want to say,
Thank you for being there for me every day Daddy,
Thank you for making me have fun,
Thank you for everything you have done,
Thank you for always helping me out,
Thank you for making me realise what life is all about,
*I love you, Daddy!*

Jacqueline Wallace (13)
Lomond School, Helensburgh

# That's My Dad

Baby minder
Nappy changer
Swing pusher
Road runner
Hill walker
Dog walker
Sea diver
Horse groomer
Beer drinker
Family lover
Law keeper
Advice giver
Big hugger
Omelette maker
Bacon eater
Car washer
Bike rider
Heavy snorer
Music listener
Cigar smoker
Dinner maker
Sport supporter
Prayer speaker
Loving father
That's my dad!

Emma Wilson (13)
Lomond School, Helensburgh

# A Nice Day With My Dad

One fine summer's day my dad and I,
Took a trip to the Isle of Skye,
We were looking for otters and other wildlife too,
The sea around Skye was a very deep blue.
The air was fresh and summer was definitely there,
My dad was impressed when I spotted an otter quite near.
It was a lot of fun and we had a great laugh,
And once I got home I had a warm bath.
You are funny and kind,
You have a fast car,
You put yourself after others,
You're great, you really are.
You are the best a dad could be,
You're nice to everyone not just me.
It was such a great day in every single way,
And I'd just like to wish you a Happy Father's Day!

Jennifer Craig (13)
Lomond School, Helensburgh

# The Dad I Have

The dad I have is smart and funny,
He takes us out and complains about the money.
He watches football, cricket too
And then wonders what else to do.
He makes a mess and leaves it there,
Until my mum gives him that evil stare.
He laughs about it then looks in the mirror
Remembering the boxer he was the other year.
He asks us silly questions he knows we won't understand
And because of that he thinks he's right grand.
But he's only messing, he wouldn't hurt a fly,
He's a big, gentle giant with sensitive eyes.
He's kind and knows how to have a laugh,
I'm very grateful for the dad I have.

Chantelle Gale (14)
Rodillian School, Wakefield

# My Ideal Dad

My ideal dad is the one
Who never shouts
He's smart and funny
And you never see him frown

He always gives me money
Even takes me to town
He always takes my side
And lifts me when I'm down

That's my ideal dad
The one I haven't got
You see I have a dad
But he's not as cool as that!

Luke Shields (14)
Rodillian School, Wakefield

# My Dad At The Shops

When my dad goes shopping
Nothing's ever right
He goes to get some bread
But ends up there all night

When my dad goes shopping
Everything goes wrong
He goes to get some boxer shorts
But comes back with a thong

When my dad goes shopping
Nothing's ever right
He gets the wrong cereal
And ends up in a fight.

Liam Elliott (14)
Rodillian School, Wakefield

# The Perfect Fit

If dads were sold in the thousands,
And you could buy them in the shops like shoes,
My dad would be perfect Gucci knock-offs,
Ones I'd always use.
I'd wear them out,
I'd scuff them and scrape them,
And not notice at all,
Until one day,
The heels could break,
And I would simply fall.
I know I shouldn't take my shoes for granted,
It's not every day you find something so perfect
For such a little price to pay,
But even if my dad is a pair of broken, knock-off shoes,
He's the best fit I'll ever find
And that really is OK!

Danya Leanne Wilson (14)
Rodillian School, Wakefield

# The World's Worst Dad

The world's worst dad
Would be a dad who could not tie his shoes
And when he eats his meals he eats them with a straw.
When he does some DIY the house falls to the floor.
All my dad ever does is eat all day
So when we go to a restaurant he screams,
'All you can eat buffet.'

Nathan Kane (13)
Rodillian School, Wakefield

# Mark, My Dad

Mark with a K
That's my dad
I'm Marc with a C.

Mark with a K's
A tiler by trade
Wants me to follow.

Marc with a C
Has different ideas
He wants a sporting career.

Marc Gaunt (14)
Rodillian School, Wakefield

# My Dad

My dad is crazy
My dad is mad
My dad likes his whisky
Because it gets him tipsy

My dad is cool
Because he knows how to use a tool
My dad is a boy racer in his Skyline.

Danny Rochelle (14)
Rodillian School, Wakefield

# Everyone Needs A Dad

Everyone needs a dad to love.
Everyone needs a dad to be loved by.
Everyone needs a dad they can trust.
Everyone needs a dad that they can be trusted by.
Everyone needs a dad for life.
Everyone needs a dad that will want you for life.
Everyone needs a dad!

Lauren Lyth (13)
Rodillian School, Wakefield

# My Super Dad!

My super dad, he loves football.
My super dad, he works for Spar.
My super dad, he loves Leeds United.
My super dad, he lays on the sofa all day long.
My super dad, he is my mate.
He is ace.
I love my dad.

Thomas While (13)
Rodillian School, Wakefield

# Through The Baby's Eyes

Who's this stranger looking at me?
He picks me up and cuddles me, warm as can be.
He looks at me with great awe
And all I want to say to him is,
'Cuddle me once more.'
But all that comes out is *goo, goo, goo.*
Then he says he's talking to me
*Coochi, coochi, coo*
Now this is quite annoying
And rather stupid too
And if this is all he's gonna do
I'd rather live in a zoo
But then he says he loves me
And that touches me deep
But that's the last thing I heard
Cos then I went to sleep.
When I woke slowly
From my greatest sleep
He whispers in my ear,
'You're my son which forever I will keep.'

John Skerrett (13)
Rodillian School, Wakefield

# Ideal Dad

If I could make my ideal dad
I would make him so
He was never sad
I would make him so
He was always glad
I would make him so
He would never cry
I would make him so
He would not be shy
I would make him so
He'd shine like the sun
I would make him so
He's always fun
I would make him so
He's always great
And he'll be my bestest mate!

Carlie Sanderson  (13)
Rodillian School, Wakefield

# Vampire Dads

My dad's a vampire
He stays out at night
He drinks blood of the living
And stores some in the fridge

My dad's a vampire
He only eats meat
The blood drips, drops and splutters
On the stony floor

My dad's a vampire
He can be really scary
He's got no reflection
Though he still says he looks pretty good

My dad's a vampire
He is as bald as a vulture
His fangs are as long as windscreen wipers
Though he says he's normal.

My dad's a vampire
What's yours?

Adam Sellers (13)
Rodillian School, Wakefield

# What Is A Dad?

A dad's the guy who's
Always there.
The guy you know will
Always care.
You'll see him on a morning.
You'll see him on a night.
But how important is
He in your life?

When you're hurting he'll
Feel your pain.
He'd choose you over fortune
And fame.
Sometimes you say that
He's embarrassing.
But you know without him
Life wouldn't be the same.

He buys you presents and spoils
You mad.
He hates to scold you if you're bad.
To protect you he'd give up his life.
He'd shield you from danger, he'd
Fight your fight.

A dad's the guy who's always there.
The guy you know will always care.
You'll see him on a morning. You'll
See him on a night.
But how important is he in your life?

Rachel Morley (14)
Rodillian School, Wakefield

# The Perfect Dad

The perfect dad would always be there.
The perfect dad would always care.
The perfect dad would take you anywhere.
The perfect dad would spoil you rotten.
The perfect dad would let you stay in bed all day.
It's a bad job the perfect dad doesn't exist really.

Isobel Robinson (13)
Rodillian School, Wakefield

# Super Dad

In the day he is normal.
He sits and drinks his tea.
He wears his slippers.
He watches TV.

But at night he's different.
He fights off evil.
Protecting me and you.
He saves the world from destruction.

My dad's a superhero.
He wears the suit too.
He always eats his greens.
He's pathetic when he gets flu.

In the day he is normal.

Kelvin Stott (14)
Rodillian School, Wakefield

# Normal

He's not dumb
He's not smart
He always takes the mick
His habits, don't get me started

He doesn't get drunk
He's not rich
But almost skint
Yet he still provides

He's always busy
But still helps out
He's more like a friend
That's why he is the opposite to *normal!*

Nathan Rose (13)
Rodillian School, Wakefield

# My Dad Is ...

My dad is a superhero
He flies to the pub.
My dad is a detective
He finds out everything I've done.
My dad is a music critic
He listens to a load of pap.
My dad is a racer
He loves fast cars.
My dad is a comedian
He always makes me laugh.
My dad is a businessman
He always talks about work.
My dad is my dad
And I wouldn't change him at all.

Alexander Durow (14)
Rodillian School, Wakefield

# My Ideal Dad!

My ideal dad would be
A great man.
A man with great
Ambitions.
My ideal dad would be
A cool man.
A man with lots of style.
My ideal dad would be
A dad that never said no.

But I don't want an ideal dad
I love him the way he is!

Sarah Frearson (14)
Rodillian School, Wakefield

# Fishing

Why is it dads always think they're best at fishing?

Kids always ask them what they've caught
They say they have caught a monster
But really we know they haven't
So we just play along with the act

They always buy the best rods
Because they think it makes them better
But really it just costs a lot
And doesn't make them better

When kids go with their dads fishing
The dads are always wishing
That they finally catch one this time
But it's always the kids that do

When dads catch nothing
They always blame their equipment
They go and buy a new rod
And the mums always go mad.

Why is it dads always think they're best at fishing?

Gemma Packer (14)
Rodillian School, Wakefield

# Why I Love My Dad

My dad sings
My dad laughs
He has a pint
Then gets a bath
He talks about music
He talks about football
He complains about loud music
And complains about the TV.

He complains about untidiness
And never understands me
So that's why I love my dad.

When I am out he shouts me
When I run he catches me
And when I laugh he laughs with me.
That's why I love my dad.

When I am tired or upset
He jumps out and cuddles me
So that's why I love my dad.

If I dance or sing
Or even jump and shout out everything
He makes me warm
And he compliments me.
That's why I love my dad.

Natalie Hughes (13)
Rodillian School, Wakefield

# Dads

My dad
  He is really, really cool.
Your dad,
  He is really, really uncool.
My dad,
  He is really, really tall.
Your dad,
  He is really, really short.
My dad,
  He is really, really funny.
Your dad,
  He is really, really unfunny.
My dad,
  He is really, really loving.
Your dad,
  He is really, really unloving.
My dad,
  He is really, really skinny.
Your dad,
  He is really, really fat.
My dad,
  Is the best.
Your dad,
  Is the worst.

Josh Bennett (12)
Rodillian School, Wakefield

# Dad And His Tools

Oh no, here we go again,
Dad's back with his tools.
He's always telling me and Mum,
Next to him that Handy Andy's a fool.

I come back home to lie on my bed,
But find that it's been changed.
Into a birdhouse and a workbench,
I think he's gone deranged.

He's always wanting buckets,
But I'm not too sure what for.
Because every time he goes to the car boot,
He seems to bring back more.

A great thing about my dad,
Is that he's like this fountain of knowledge.
When he helps me with my homework,
He's like my own personal college.

But I never want to in my life,
See another drill.
If that horrible sound wakes me up again,
I'll go in for the kill.

Chris Day (13)
Rodillian School, Wakefield

# I'm Glad You're My Dad

You shout at me and I shout back
But I'm glad you're my dad.

You taught me how to kick a ball
When I was very small.

You explained the offside rule to me
But didn't make much sense age 3.

You held the bike whilst I learnt to ride
I was glad you were by my side.

Relatives say I looked like you
Does that mean I have grey hair too?

Although we tend to disagree
You are the dad for me.

*Chris Timms (12)*
Rodillian School, Wakefield

# Dad, You're Really Annoying

Dad, you're really annoying me!
So shut your mouth!

When you drill it leaves a massive hole
That looks like a football.

My dad wears a crown
But looks like a clown.

My dad is a fat elephant
And looks like an apple hat.

My dad is a whinger
Who has a long fringe.

But my dad is really a wonderful dad.

*Jonathan Rayner (13)*
Rodillian School, Wakefield

# My Dad

My dad makes me laugh.
He helps me with my homework.
My dad thinks he's the best
But really he's not.

My dad makes me laugh
But he always talks daft.
My dad is kind
And so am I.

My dad makes me laugh.
He takes me places
Where I want to go
And buys me new coats.

My dad makes me laugh
And whatever I say
He's my dad.

*Kirsty Hall (12)*
Rodillian School, Wakefield

# The Day At Scarborough

We were only in Scarborough a minute
My dad had already kicked off
A stupid man started on him
So he gave him the lot.

We tried to park at the front
But they sent us to the back
My dad used his charm
And got us first class.

We went on the beach
And a crab bit my dad's feet
We all started laughing
And my dad started shouting.

It turned 3 o'clock
It was time to pick up the rock
Then we hit the road
Returning from a super trip.

Hayley Kershaw (13)
Rodillian School, Wakefield

# My Dad And Family

Never in, always at golf
Stuck at the 19th hole
If he's not at golf he's cleaning for Mum
He thinks he's hilarious but he can be funny.

My dad may shout, I might shout back
When I was little my dad taught me to ride
And I remember when my dad was crying
When Leanne's rabbit died.

When I was 2 I broke my arm
My dad was there supporting me
Sometimes my family say I look like him
Does that mean I look like a man?

The best of all I love him with all my heart
And he's all mine.

Emma Haynes (13)
Rodillian School, Wakefield

# My Dad's The King!

When he comes home, my dad's the king,
He showers us with presents!
He pretends that he knows everything,
But we ask him and he's hesitant.

He sits atop his sofa throne,
And orders for his slippers.

When he comes home, my dad's the boss,
We have to do his ironing,
If we don't then he gets cross,
But it's so very tiring.

He sits atop his sofa throne
And commands for the remote.

When he comes home, my dad's my dad,
I'll love him wherever he is,
When he's away, I miss him a tad,
But his jokes are hit and miss.

Kimberley Bourne (13)
Rodillian School, Wakefield

# My Poem About My Dad Called Steven

My dad has spikes on his head
And thinks that he is in fashion,
But really he is a geek.
He thinks that he can dance
But really he is rubbish.
If I am naughty he will slap me
And tell me to sit in a chair
And don't move.
He is always moaning that he is putting on weight
And I keep telling him it's because he eats a lot.
Sometimes he is funny
But is daft and goes mad
When it comes to doing my homework.
But after all he is my dad
And that is all that matters.

*Jessica Hartley (13)*
Rodillian School, Wakefield

# Vampire Dad

My dad is a vampire,
He hides in the mud,
And when he sees people,
He drinks all their blood!

I used to have a friend,
He once brought round his cat,
But when we were playing,
Dad ate it on the mat!

My dad has a comfy coffin,
But doesn't sleep all night,
He goes out on a rampage,
And doesn't come in till light!

I once got something on my dad's cloak,
It really made a stain,
He tried to wash it very well,
After he whipped me with a cane!

What a brilliant dad!

*Ethan Turnor (13)*
Rodillian School, Wakefield

# My Dad

My dad likes dogs
My dad likes building and making things
My dad loves his car
My dad loves spending money on his car
My dad likes to drink
My dad loves to watch TV
My dad hates shopping
My dad likes his ferrets
My dad loves to drive
My dad's favourite word is bed.

Joshua Brockley (12)
Rodillian School, Wakefield

# My Dad

My dad is sometimes funny
But not as often as he thinks he is.

My dad smokes
But I wish he would stop.

My dad loves a pint
But sometimes goes too far.

My dad loves gardening
And is really good.

My dad loves shopping
But buys a lot of rubbish.

My dad loves walking the dog
But sometimes the dog walks him.

My dad loves football
But is no good at playing it.

Sarah Hazel (12)
Rodillian School, Wakefield

# My Dad

My dad thinks he is funny
But he is not

My dad loves gardening
He even talks to the plants

My dad is all-day annoying
And all day snoring

My dad loves curry
He has it every Friday

My dad needs to grow up
We have competitions who goes in the new shower more

My dad dances like a chicken
But he thinks he dances like Usher or something

All the bad things he does
Will never change the fact that I love him.

Heather Pickering (11)
Rodillian School, Wakefield

# My Dad

My dad is funny and good at driving
My dad is a wagon driver
My dad likes dogs
My dad thinks he's a boy racer on the motorway
My dad likes gardening
My dad needs to stop smoking
My dad is brave
My dad thinks he's cool but he looks like someone out of the 80s
He doesn't like shopping
My dad likes playing football
My dad likes his job
My dad likes watching TV.

Sam Audsley (11)
Rodillian School, Wakefield

# My Dad

My dad is funny.
My dad drives an RAC van and a Mitsubishi land rover.
My dad hates food and clothes shopping.
My dad breaks the law.
By going 40mph in a 30mph speed limit zone.
My dad needs to pay his maintenance on time.
My dad needs to slow down on the motorway and major roads.
My dad likes his job in the RAC.
My dad doesn't spend his money as much.
My dad doesn't like doing the gardening.
My dad doesn't like football or watching it on the TV.
My dad is lazy.

Charlie Rowley (12)
Rodillian School, Wakefield

# The Best Kind Of Guy

My dad's small but full of heart,
And he's been with me from the start.

He's there for me in time of need,
Except when watching rugby league!

The time we spend is well spent,
And when we are together he's a real gent.

He makes me laugh, he makes me cry,
But all in all he's the *best* kind of guy!

Rebecca Field (13)
Rodillian School, Wakefield

# Me And My Dad

My dad has a go at me
I have a go back
He says I am stupid
I say that he is daft
He tells me to shut up
He tells me what to do
But I love him through and through

He has a laugh with me
I have a laugh back
He helps me with my homework
He explains to me the maths
He buys me presents
He is good to me
That's why I love him
And he loves me.

**Danny Roberts (13)**
Rodillian School, Wakefield

# My Dad

My dad is quite funny,
He always has a laugh,
He thinks he's a good dancer,
But he is rather naff!

My dad makes me laugh,
He can't do DIY,
He isn't a very good fighter,
And if he tried he would get a black eye!

That's when it gets embarrassing,
He doesn't fight like me,
I'm a lot harder than my dad,
So he tries to be like me!

Jade Chappell (13)
Rodillian School, Wakefield

# My Embarrassing Dad

My dad's so embarrassing
That every time someone comes round:
He shows them my baby pictures.
He dances about in his knickers.
He sings when he can't even sing.
My dad's so embarrassing.

Well, my dad's so embarrassing
That when we go out he:
Puts his arm around me and skips.
He picks out baby clothes for me
And says this is cute when people are looking.
He even sings in public.
My dad's more embarrassing.

My dad's so embarrassing
That when he takes me to school he:
Winds the window down and shouts, 'Be careful,'
And 'have a good time, honey.'
He straightens my clothes
And re-does my tie when people are looking.
He even shouts, 'Love you,'
And gives me a lunch.
Why are dads so embarrassing?

Bethany Morley (11)
Rodillian School, Wakefield

# The Ape In My Dad

I'm sure there's an ape in my dad;
He slouches his back.
He hangs around the house
And goes absolutely spare,
And loves a banana or two.
He's bald on top with a bit at the edge
With big, great hands
He gives me a cuddle.

Katie Greening (12)
Rodillian School, Wakefield

# A Dad's Purpose!

A dad's purpose is
To push his children
On the swing at noon.

A dad's purpose is
To camp out with his son
And watch clouds pass the moon.

A dad's purpose is
To watch TV
And go into a trance.

A dad's purpose is
To watch his little girl grow up
And learn how to dance.

But my dad is here to be
My cool dad.

*Kimberley Richardson (11)*
Rodillian School, Wakefield

# World's Best Dad

My dad takes me to the matches,
He's the world's best dad.

He talks about the rhinos,
He's the world's best dad.

He sometimes buys me pressies,
He's the world's best dad.

They're always full of love,
He's the world's best dad.

*He's the world's best dad.*

Chloe Coggill (11)
Rodillian School, Wakefield

# About My Dad

My dad is the best
He's my best friend, sometimes not
But he still loves me

My dad is very lazy
Sleeps all day on a Sunday
He is very, very lazy

My dad is the best
He's my best friend, sometimes not
But he still loves me

Sometimes he plays cards
On the computer he stays
Until my mum says

My dad is the best
He's my best friend, sometimes not
But he still loves me

Acts like a little boy
Now he plays on the PoCo
Every day from now

My dad is the best
He's my best friend, sometimes not
But he still loves me

Mum makes his breakfast
Tomorrow and every morning
She even makes his supper

My dad is the best
He's my best friend, sometimes not
But I still love him

My dad is very lazy
And that is a fact
I will always love him.

Kayleigh Pearson (12)
Rodillian School, Wakefield

# A Christmas Wish

Everyone makes a wish
I made a Christmas wish one day
But I didn't think it would come true
The wish I made was a Christmas wish

Think what was your number 1 wish
I got the choice and I chose a dad
A dad just for me
And that was my wish come true

I got a dad who I thought was the best
Better than all the rest
He bought me presents that I thought I'd never get
He brought me up as one of his own

He brought to the family a sister
Just for me
And that is the best pressie to me

My dad is called David
He is really special to me.

Kristen Krysiak (12)
Rodillian School, Wakefield

# Dads

Dads are excellent.
Dads are great.
Whenever I think of my dad
I smile.

Dads are excellent.
Dads are great.
Whenever I think of my dad
I wanna cry.

Dads are excellent.
Dads are great.
Whenever my dad's around
I smile.

Dads are excellent.
Dads are great.
I love mine
But do you love yours?

*Kayleigh Garner (13)*
Rodillian School, Wakefield

# My Dad The Gangster

My dad's a gangster,
He thinks he's really fly,
He walks around with loads of bling,
It makes me wanna cry.

My dad's a gangster,
He thinks he's proper pimped,
He walks around with plastic guns
And says he has a limp.

My dad's a gangster
Although really he's not,
People think he's really mad,
They think he's smoking pot!

My dad's no gangster,
He really is so glum,
He has no credit cards
And no proof of income.

My dad's no gangster,
I wouldn't change him ever,
He cheers me up when I'm down,
In fact he's really clever.

Matthew Bornshin (13)
Rodillian School, Wakefield

# Imaginary Dad

I have an imaginary dad,
My real one wasn't there at birth.
I used to think I'd done something bad,
But I know he is somewhere on Earth.

I would like to find him one day,
Maybe when I am a parent myself.
I hope he knows my birthday is the first of May,
Wonder if he has asked about my health?

I am worried about finding him,
He is the father I never had.
He might have another kid named Kim,
But anyway, I love you, Dad.

Kirstie Backhouse (13)
Rodillian School, Wakefield

# The Ideal Dad

The ideal dad would be funny
The ideal dad would have a good job
The ideal dad would not be embarrassing
The ideal dad would have a good family
The ideal dad would be caring and kind
The ideal dad would be loving
The ideal dad would take you everywhere that you wanted
The ideal dad would be my dad.

Vicky Handley (12)
Rodillian School, Wakefield

# My Dad

I get some of my good points and some of my faults from my dad.
I'm strong willed, wise but I am quite loud I must add!

I am quite smart and always willing to learn,
But I sometimes shout out when it's not my turn.

I am supportive and helpful and pretty strong,
But I correct others' grammar if they are wrong.

I know I can be annoying, too honest and loud,
But I get those points from my dad so I am rather proud.

Bethany Spencer (12)
Royds School, Leeds

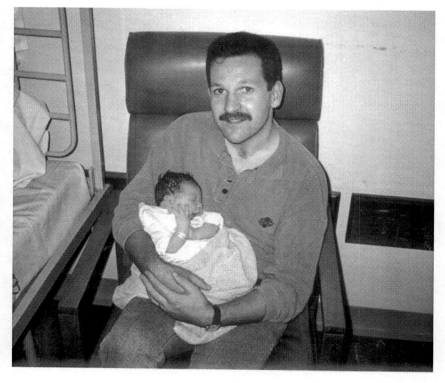

# Dad

As I woke up this morning,
I looked into the sky,
Warmth was all around me,
And the sun was flying high.

I thought of you this morning,
And remembered what you said,
You told me not to be afraid, Dad,
You showed me the path ahead.

You told me not to drink, Dad,
You told me not to smoke,
You told me all this great advice,
But I really couldn't cope.

You said you'd always be there, Dad,
You said you'd always care,
You said you'd never let me go
But your love was very rare.

I said I'd never miss you, Dad,
But that was a lie,
'Cause now it's all reality,
Oh how you make me cry!

I want you to know now, Dad,
That our love is very strong,
I want you to know now, Dad,
That our love will live on!

Jessica Dobson (14)
Royds School, Leeds

# My Dad

Smiling
Laughing dad
Rugby playing
Football kicking
Lifting me in the
Supermarket
To get the things on
The high shelf
Cuddly at night-time
My dad is the best.

Alexander Ogilvy (8)
St Leonards School, Fife

# My Daddy

My daddy is a tickly person,
when I tickle him, he laughs,
I laugh too.
He likes playing rugby and golf
and he loves motorsport.
When Daddy is in America and I
hear a lawnmower, it reminds
me of Daddy and I feel sad.
We play racing in the swimming pool
when we are in Florida.
Sometimes we play my Xbox
without Mum knowing.
I love my daddy a lot, he is
the best daddy in the world.

Jordan Hutchison (8)
St Leonards School, Fife

# My Number One Dad

Saviour to animals
World's number one dad
Smells like Lynx deodorant
I feel it's a comforting smell
He feels hairy and busy after
'A bad day at work!'
But on other days
He feels silky like a cat that has been well looked after
I miss him when he goes away
I feel like a forgotten jigsaw I can't put together
I miss his laugh, his comforting smell and his lovely feel,
He completes my jigsaw.

Bethany Ferguson (8)
St Leonards School, Fife

# My Dad

My dad is fun
As bright as the setting sun
His laughter is like a breath of fresh air
It stays with you even when he is not there
My dad is great it's plain to see
He will go down in history
He loves me and I love him
He would help me at a whim!

Jake Boyle (11)
Star of the Sea RC Primary School, Whitley Bay

# My Dad

He's bouncy and funny,
Lovely and jubberly,
He's always in a happy mood!
He likes to play on Saturday
While scoffing all the food!

His name is Walt,
But he doesn't care
Even though he's hardly got hair.

He's cool and he rules,
He has moves in the pool
And I'm always glad he's my dad!

Jack Swann (11)
Star of the Sea RC Primary School, Whitley Bay

# My Dad Is Fab

**M** agnificent at telling bad jokes
**Y** et always making me laugh

**D** efinitely the best
**A** mazing at everything
**D** ancing of his is embarrassing

**I** wouldn't change him for the world though
**S** pecial in every way

**F** antastic is he
**A** stounding is he
**B** est by far, I love him lots.

*Rosie Marriott (11)*
Star of the Sea RC Primary School, Whitley Bay

# My Dad

My dad is the best
And you don't know him
He's much better than the rest!
He's the coolest you could imagine
But he's mine, not to share!

Richard Stobbart (11)
Star of the Sea RC Primary School, Whitley Bay

# My Dad

My dad is the best
Better than the rest
Always making me laugh -
His terrible cooking
Burnt toast from the toaster
Yet my dad is the best.

Jonathan Murphy (11)
Star of the Sea RC Primary School, Whitley Bay

# If My Dad Were A Strong Man

If my dad were a strong man,
Life would be so cool.
He'd throw me up a hundred feet,
When we were in the pool.

If my dad were a strong man,
I'd have no enemies.
Everyone would be scared of him,
Including big bullies.

My dad's not a strong man,
But I love him all the same.
And if anyone replaces him,
I'll stick them down the drain.

Joseph Steven Jeffrey (11)
Star of the Sea RC Primary School, Whitley Bay

# My Dad

My dad is kind
He likes to drink
He is quite good at helping out.

My dad can drive
But cannot sing
And works for a company called Transco.

He sometimes jokes
He's sometimes sad
But he will always be my dad.

Joseph Mould (11)
Star of the Sea RC Primary School, Whitley Bay

# Dad, Dad, Where Have You Gone?

Dad, Dad, I can't go to bed
Dad, Dad, I'm scared of the dark
Dad, Dad, these pyjamas are too big
Dad, Dad, you're the best

Dad, Dad, the light's switched off
Dad, Dad, it's really spooky
Dad, Dad, I need your help
Dad, Dad, you're the best

Dad, Dad, I know you love it in Africa
But the windows are open
The curtains are blowing
And it looks like a ghost

There's a spider on my bed
It's coming right up to me
And it's really, really big
It's coming right up to me
So please come soon.

*Joseph Hakin (9)*
Star of the Sea RC Primary School, Whitley Bay

# Dad's Favourite Poem

Once there was my dad
Sitting like he was mad
Saying goodbye
To his pie
As he sleeps on the cosy settee fast asleep
Dreaming down quite deep
When he wakes up he gets a fright
Of the horrible bad dream, that's right
When he felt better he had a cup of tea
He thinks that makes him stronger by eating peas
He thinks he's funny
When he likes cute little bunnies.

Zarius Ferozepurwalla (9)
Star of the Sea RC Primary School, Whitley Bay

# Dad, You Are The Best

**M** y dad is cool
**Y** ou know how much he rules

**D** ad takes me to the swimming pool
**A** nd even if he sometimes is a fool
**D** addy, you know how much you need a rest
**D** ad, you're the best
**Y** ou are even better than a puffed teddy bear

**I** s your dad very loving?
**S** o if he is he must be very lovely.

There is one thing I want to tell you
It is that my dad is ...
Cool and he should rule this school!

*Madeline Masters (9)*
Star of the Sea RC Primary School, Whitley Bay

# Number One Dad

**N** ice and caring to me and family
**U** nusual and humorous
**M** agical and amazing for everyone
**B** etter than all the rest you'll see
**E** xciting and loving
**R** oaring with laughter all the time

**O** ver and over again he takes me out
**N** o matter with glasses and no hair at all
**E** mbarrassing he has been with little Ed at his side

**D** elightful and daring always is he
**A** life he has as an engineer
**D** efinitely my number one dad!

Holly Swann (9)
Star of the Sea RC Primary School, Whitley Bay

# Number One Dad

Dad, Dad, you are the best
You are better than the rest,
Dad, Dad, you're really cool
Dad, Dad, you really rule.

Dad, Dad, you drive a car
Dad, Dad, you are a star,
Dad, Dad, I love you so
I just want you to know

*You rock!*

Daniel Mould (9)
Star of the Sea RC Primary School, Whitley Bay

# My Dad

My dad is the best
He won't sell me for a vest,
After a day at school
He'll take me to the swimming pool.

When he has made some food
He'll say I'm his dude,
When I'm playing with my van
He says I'm his little man.

My dad is not at old age
I write down on this page,
My dad hates Power Rangers
He likes TV dangers.

I am very glad
That I have my dad,
He is not at all bad
And he is still my dad.

Alexander Chidambaram (9)
Star of the Sea RC Primary School, Whitley Bay

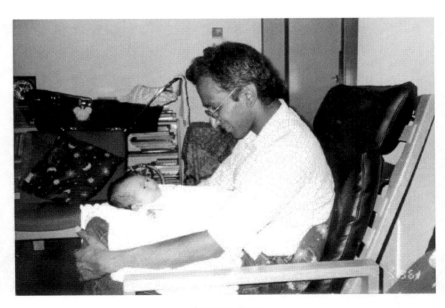

# My Dad

My dad is the best
My dad beats all the rest
My dad is not lazy
And he is not crazy.

My dad likes beer
My dad likes deer
My dad is funny
And he likes Bugs Bunny.

My dad goes to work
He is not a jerk
My dad likes to play
And he shouts, 'Yeehay!'

My dad is cool
He goes in the swimming pool
My dad is fun
He lies in the sun.

My dad goes to see his mum
And goes for a sticky bun
My dad is not mean
And he likes green.

You rock, Dad!

Thomas Chapman (9)
Star of the Sea RC Primary School, Whitley Bay

# My Daddy

**M** is for all the money that he gives me
**Y** is for the yellowness in his room.

**D** is for all the dinners he makes me
**A** is for the arms he still cuddles me with
**D** is for all the desserts I help him to make
**D** is for the dadness, he wouldn't get rid of me
**Y** is for all the yo-yos he has bought me.

I wouldn't change him for the world
He's the number one daddy!

*Bethany Abbott (9)*
Star of the Sea RC Primary School, Whitley Bay

# My Dad

My dad, he's the best
Me and my dad do lots of fun things together
My dad takes me to castles and I love it
He lets me climb and he buys me an ice cream.

My dad, he's the best
My brother loves Dad, so do I
He plays with me and my brother
At night I say, 'Dad, Dad, sing me a song.'

My dad, he's the best
He helps me
And when I am sad he is too
So when I am happy he's happy.

My dad, he's the best
He likes beer
And I love my dad very much
And he loves me.

Kirsten McIlduff (9)
Star of the Sea RC Primary School, Whitley Bay

# Better Than The Rest!

My dad is the best, better than the rest,
He takes seven ties to work,
He puts them in his drawer and does some paperwork,
My dad needs the phone all the time
And the computer too,
We get annoyed at that
But who cares?
We always do!

My dad is the best, better than the rest,
My dad is full of love and happiness too,
He's better than all the other dads,
Yes, your dads.

Rachael Coady
Star of the Sea RC Primary School, Whitley Bay

# My Dad (Haiku)

My dad is a king
No dad is better than mine
My dad is a king.

Simeon Conway (11)
Star of the Sea RC Primary School, Whitley Bay

# My Dad

**M** y dad is the best
**Y** et is very funny

**D** ad rules all the time
**A** nd he plays guitar
**D** efinitely the best.

Michael Oates
Star of the Sea RC Primary School, Whitley Bay

# My Dad!

My dad likes beer
He goes to the match and starts to cheer
When we score he goes really mad
Sometimes I say, 'Shut up, Dad!'
At half-time everyone stares
And he says nobody cares

Sometimes he can be so boring
Watching tennis and starts snoring
My dad loves Coke
And some people say, 'What a weird bloke.'

Ben Murphy (9)
Star of the Sea RC Primary School, Whitley Bay

# My Dad

**M** is for the music which he loves to play.
**Y** is for *yippee!* which I cry when he comes in from work each day.

**D** is for the yummy dinners which he cooks.
**A** is for Annemarie, his wife, whom he loves.
**D** is for my dad who I love *so* much!

Áine Beldon (11)
Star of the Sea RC Primary School, Whitley Bay

# My Dad

My dad is so kind
And nice and cool
He has black hair
And a big laugh too

He is so funny
And a bit wild
He has green eyes
And a very big smile

His name is John
My little cousins
Call him Scone
And I wouldn't change him for the world.

*Ryder Buchanan (11)*
Star of the Sea RC Primary School, Whitley Bay

# A Father Is ...

A father is a good effort that looks after the family.
My father wants to be better
But I don't think he can be.
He's fine how he is.
He feeds my tummy
And loves my mummy
Yet doesn't think about himself.
He's so funny and sneezes like honey
And has a bath every other day.
He works in the house just like a mouse
Without being seen or heard.
A father is someone to look up to
So we get the picture
A father is all we need.

Tom Hakin (10)
Star of the Sea RC Primary School, Whitley Bay

# My Dad Is ...

My dad is kind
He has a very clever mind
He's also funny
And has a very flat tummy

My dad is caring
And always sharing
He makes me smile
He has a very funky style

My dad kisses and cuddles me
He loves me and that's easy to see
He has a very caring touch
And I love him very, very much.

Victoria Alice Marriott (6)
Star of the Sea RC Primary School, Whitley Bay

# Poem For My Dad

My dad is very crazy
He can sometimes be lazy
Every night he eats his tea
Then he tries to tickle me
He plays games with my brother and me
He can be quite silly you see
I love him a lot
He's the best dad I've got.

Hannah Chapman (6)
Star of the Sea RC Primary School, Whitley Bay

# The Roles Of 'Dad'

The kind, funny, generous man,
I have known him all my life
The one who loves to read books
Watch Laurel and Hardy, listen to country songs.
You may be thinking, who is this person I speak of?
My wonderful grandad of course!

A tormentor, the sarcastic one
Also funny, kind and generous.
There are two sides to him.
Just loves to have a break
And go on holidays, laze around.
You may be thinking, who is this person I speak of?
My fantastic dad of course!

Hannah Marnell (11)
The Blue Coat School, Wavertree

# Information

We hope you have enjoyed reading this book - and that you will continue to enjoy it in the coming years. If you like reading and writing poems and stories drop us a line, or give us a call, and we'll send you a free information pack.

**Write to**
**Young Writers, Remus House, Coltsfoot Drive,**
**Woodston, Peterborough PE2 9JX**
**(01733) 890066**

**Alternatively check out our website:**
**www.youngwriters.co.uk**